The Craft of
Modal Counterpoint

A Practical Approach

Thomas Benjamin

SCHIRMER BOOKS

A Division of Macmillan Publishing Co., Inc.

NEW YORK

Collier Macmillan Publishers

LONDON

This book is dedicated to my parents,
Paul and Frances,
and to my wife, Liz.

Schirmer Books
A Division of Macmillan Publishing Co., Inc.
866 Third Avenue, New York, N.Y. 10022

Collier Macmillan Canada, Ltd.

Library of Congress Catalog Card Number: 77-90012

Printed in the United States of America

printing number
2 3 4 5 6 7 8 9 10

Library of Congress Cataloging in Publication Data

Benjamin, Thomas.
   The craft of modal counterpoint.

   Bibliography: p.
   Includes index.
   1. Counterpoint. I. Title.
MT55.B447   781.4'2   77-90012
ISBN 0-02-870480-0

Acknowledgments

Thanks are owed my students of counterpoint over the past few years for their willingness to serve as guinea pigs for several successive versions of this text and for their helpful criticisms. Drs. Robert Lynn and Robert Nelson of the University of Houston were painstaking and perceptive in their comments on the text, and the author is also grateful for helpful suggestions from Herbert Fromm. Gratitude is due Christine Womack for manuscript preparation, Anne Walters for translations, Helen Garrett for proofreading, and Reynaldo Ochoa for music copying.

The University of Houston Central Campus Publications Committee has supported this publication with a generous grant to cover music copying costs, for which I am most grateful.

Thomas Benjamin
Houston, Texas

Contents

Introduction

The basic considerations of contrapuntal craftsmanship are in essence the same for all linearly oriented music, whether that of Machaut, Bach, or Hindemith: linear clarity, directionality, and independence of line, some degree of intervallic control, textural contrast, and coordination of the vertical and horizontal elements. The differences between the earlier and later contrapuntal styles lie primarily in meter (and rhythm), texture (sonority), and balance of harmonic and melodic tendencies. The study of a predominantly linear style can function as a corrective to the often too vertical orientation of many theory courses, which tend to equate music and harmony.

It is certainly possible to base the study of counterpoint on other music, but the Palestrina style presents a model of clarity, consistency, and economy of means unrivaled by other styles. The degree of commonality in materials and techniques between composers of this period is amazing; one finds here a truly international "common practice." In its balance, poise, and avoidance of obtrusive or extraneous dramatic effects, late Renaissance sacred vocal polyphony is the perfect model of a "classic" style. The secular vocal music of the period is often as beautiful, but since it is less consistently linear and imitative this text will concentrate on the sacred style.

Once one has settled on a stylistic framework, it is necessary to decide upon an appropriate pedagogical approach. It is axiomatic that the study of any music should be based on an aural familiarity with the music under discussion. You are therefore urged to become familiar with the music of Palestrina and his contemporaries. In a classroom setting, the first few classes might best be devoted to listening to recordings, or better still to singing, as well as to discussion and investigation of the cultural and historical background. This book contains a great deal of representative music, both complete and in excerpt. It is hoped that the class will be large enough that four- and five-part music can be performed, perhaps with the help of such instruments as recorders and viols. All the music that is to be analyzed *must* be heard, and all student exercises should be performed in class. The piano should be used as little as possible, since it tends to obscure the individuality of lines.

To the Instructor

In the interest of efficiency, this text does not enter into a detailed discussion of such matters as historical music notation, performance practice, *musica ficta*, modal history and theory, the development of polyphony, the lives or output of composers, original sources, cultural and political trends in the Renaissance, and so on. It is suggested that the first few class meetings be spent investigating these matters and any other ancillary topics selected by the instructor, as well as in singing Gregorian chants and the music of the late Renaissance. The bibliography may be consulted for this purpose.

The singing and analysis of music is of the greatest importance. One can master the "rules" of any style and yet be unable to reproduce it because of inadequate familiarity with its *sound*. The alternative is to burden student and teacher with a mass of style criteria, an approach both mechanical and inefficient. It is hoped that each class will include some singing, or at least some listening. If modern practical editions are used, the instructor will need to explain the transcriptive and editorial procedures followed, in order to avoid misconceptions.

All student writing should be performed in class, and the students should be expected to do most of the criticizing. The use of multiple copies (photocopied or dittoed) or an overhead projector and work at the blackboard will greatly facilitate communication. It will be noted that this text eschews the species as inherently unmusical.* The attempt has been made to preserve the advantages of the species (a systematic approach to problems of dissonance control) by providing a series of carefully graded exercises in analysis, guided discussion, error-spotting, and written work calling for varying degrees of creativity. The exercises have been constructed so as to achieve a *musical* result even at the earliest stages, and the discussion of student writing should therefore focus not only on "correctness" but on stylistic accuracy and musicality, especially with regard to the musical line and its rhythm. More exercises are offered here than most classes will be able to complete in a one-semester course. It is strongly urged that the instructor and students work out in class some of the preliminary exercises in order to explore and clarify methodology. Sample motets composed by the class at the board will be an excellent model for the compositional process.

Any textbook that aims to be truly functional needs to steer a middle course between the overly simplified and the excessively detailed. For a compendious view of the theoretical and historical background of the Palestrina style, and a highly detailed analysis of the style itself, the student should be directed to *The Style of Palestrina and the Dissonance* and *Counterpoint*, both by Knud Jeppesen (see the Bibliography). The present text makes no attempt to cover the same ground again, but tries to distill, compress, and above all to present more interesting and more musical types of exercises. Furthermore, it does not base itself exclusively on the Palestrina style, but more broadly on the common practice of his contemporaries. A student wishing to focus on the music of any of these composers will thus be equipped with a proper background for such a study. In the interests of directness and leanness of approach, the author has tried to present the typical idioms of the style, and has labeled exceptional procedures as such. It is hoped that in the search for simplicity and clarity no gross oversimplifications have occurred.

*The delightfully abusive first chapter of R. O. Morris's *Contrapuntal Technique*, and the Introduction to Merritt's *Sixteenth-Century Counterpoint* make this point extremely well. See the Bibliography.

Student Preparation

This text makes the assumption that the student has a basic knowledge of tonal theory. For students without this preparation, the instructor will find that brief explanations within the context of the class discussion will suffice.

Notation

Throughout the text the half-note has been used to transcribe the minim, the unit of beat. In all complete works given in this text, the barline has been replaced by the *Mensurstrich* (mensuration-line notation, with the barline between staves), as a compromise between practical performance needs and rhythmic flexibility. Modern vocal clefs are used. Editorial *ficta* have been placed above the affected notes. Latin words in the music have been divided according to modern syllabication. It is suggested that students follow these conventions in writing out the exercises, although the instructor should feel free to employ whatever notation is preferred.

Selected Discography

I. Recordings for Pieces in the Book

Byrd
Ave verum corpus
MHS 877
Alpha SP 6021
London 5725
Argo 5226

II. Useful recordings of other motets

Byrd
Argo ZRG 659
Lyrichord 7156
Vanguard HM 7
Vanguard HM 750

Recordings for Pieces in the Book

Victoria

O magnum mysterium	MHS 634
	Angel S-36022
	Orion 7022
	L'Oiseau-Lyre SOL 270
	Lyrichord 7269
Quem vidistic, pastores	MHS 612

Palestrina

Jicut cervus	Pleiades P255
	DG ARC 2533322
	Kiw: SLD 10
Laudate dominum	DGG ARC 3182
	DGG ARC 198182
Dies sanctijicutus	Ace of Diamonds
	ADO 163
	or SOD 163
	Avante-garde AUS 128
	or 129

Useful recordings of other motets

Lasso
   Nonesuch 71084
   Argo ZRG 795
   DG ARC 2533290

Palestrina
   Counterpoint J602
   Angel S-36013
   Turnabout 34309
   Angel S-37514
   Odyssey 32160122
   Vanguard HM9

Lassus
   Qualiton LPX 11441

Victoria
   Argo ZRG 620
   Argo ZRG 570

General Stylistic Aspects Chapter 1

THE POLYPHONIC STYLE of Palestrina and his contemporaries is one of the most purely vocal styles in the history of music. No awkward instrumental idioms intrude on the smooth surface. This music is not dance-dominated, as is some secular vocal music of the time, and its feeling of meter comes not from the explicit placement of accent in each line but through subtler means. Its melodies are primarily conjunct, avoiding the large skips and triadic figures more proper to instrumental music. Above all it is subtle, achieving its expressive effects in unobtrusive ways.

Example 1

DIES SANCTIFICATUS   *Palestrina*

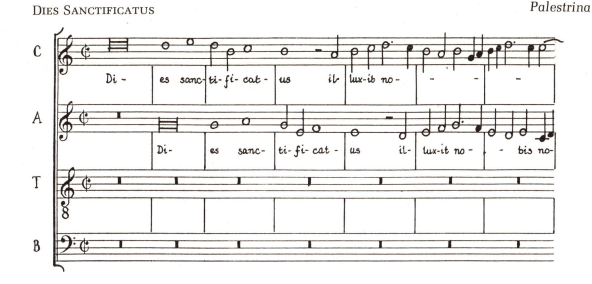

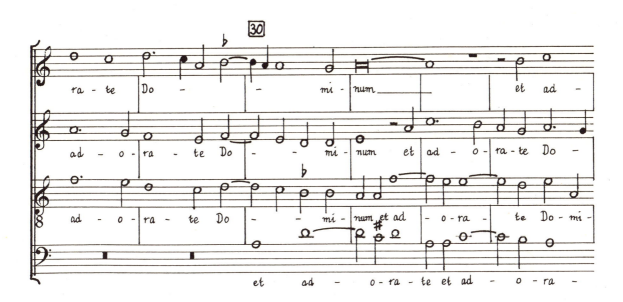

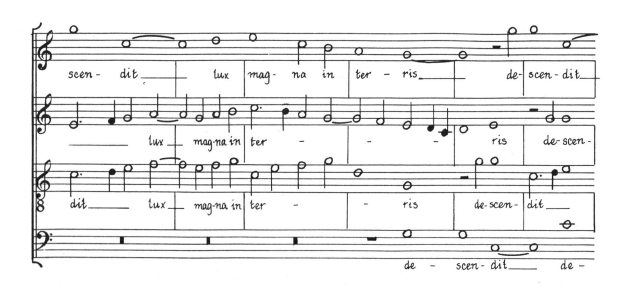

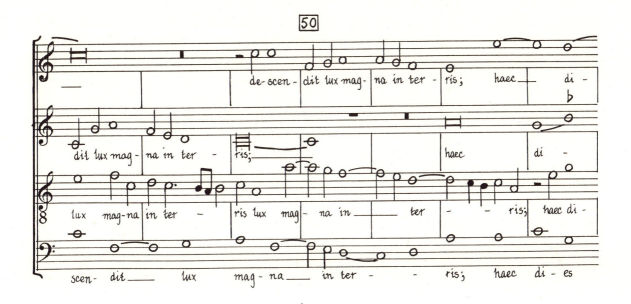

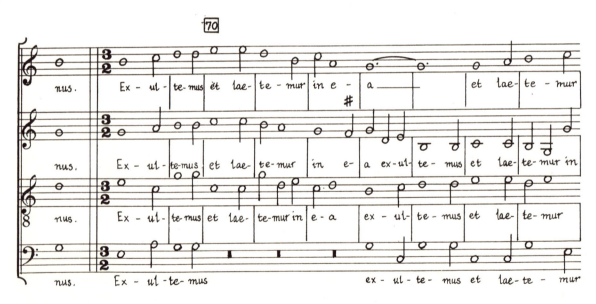

THE CRAFT OF MODAL COUNTERPOINT

A holy day has dawned for us. Come, people, and praise the Lord, for today has a great light fallen upon earth. This day has the Lord made; let us rejoice and be joyful in it.

Texture

As you have noticed in the music above, the music of Palestrina is linear in emphasis. There is no "accompaniment"; each voice is a living, independent line. Even the bass voice, while exhibiting in cadences and homophonic passages the encroachments of functional tonality, is linearly conceived and leaps only slightly more than the upper voices. Harmony results from the interaction of individual voices; it does not serve as a primary organizing force, as it often does in later music. There is little ornamentation per se in this music, although certain ornamental figures typically occur at cadence points, and there is evidence that ornaments may have been performed by singers at the time. The texture is homogeneous; there is little feeling of the treble or tenor domination that characterizes some earlier music. All the voices have about the same amount of thematic material; in imitative passages they actually have the same material. Compared to many other styles, this style is highly economical in its means, is consistent in sonority and technique, and has a restrained feeling for expression. One searches in vain here for the kind of striking dramatic effects typical of other schools and periods.

Two main textural types were employed: a contrapuntal texture, usually imitative, and a more homophonic texture, known as the *stile familiare* or familiar style. While these two are mixed freely in many works, the linear (contrapuntal) texture is more germane to the present study; we will treat the chordal (homophonic) style under four-voice texture.

The vocal ranges employed were roughly those shown below. The normal range is shown as R, and the tessitura (the heart of the range, its most useable portion) as T.

Example 2

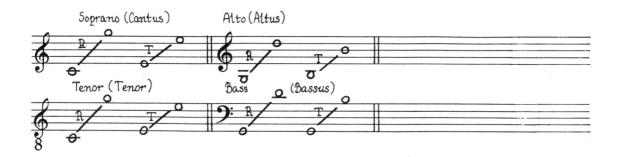

Throughout the text we will be using the arrangement of clefs shown above. Extremes of range are avoided as being awkward or obtrusive. The contrast of very high and very low is foreign to the style, as are large gaps in the middle of the texture. Adjacent voices are rarely far apart, and will occasionally cross. The thick, weighty sound of the Ockeghem school is not found here, nor is the polar texture (melody versus bass) of the Baroque. The key-word in this style is homogeneity.

Text Setting

Study the setting of the text in the motet *Dies sanctificatus*. Notice that the setting is more leisurely and drawn out than in many other kinds of music. Find the text repetitions and notice how both major and minor subdivisions of the text are articulated musically. How is accentuation achieved? How are the principal words in the text emphasized? Which note values can carry a syllable? After which note values do syllables change? Are there instances where several notes are used to set one syllable? Where does the final syllable of each section fall metrically?

An examination of text setting in sixteenth-century sacred vocal music reveals the following:

1. *Accent*. The music generally follows the accentuation of the Latin text. The important words are emphasized musically. Accent and emphasis are achieved through metric placement, height and length of note, and melismatic setting (see below). Notes that are approached by a leap, especially an ascending one, tend to sound accented.

2. *Placement of text on various note values*. Any white note can carry a syllable, unless it immediately follows a series of black notes. A single (♩) does not carry a syllable unless it is part of the figure ♩. ♩ ○; a new syllable will not otherwise follow a black note (♩). A group of black notes may carry a syllable if the syllable starts on the first note of the group, but the next syllable will not immediately follow the group.[1] A syllable is not carried by eighth notes (♪).

3. Text setting may be *syllabic* (one note per syllable), *melismatic* (many notes per syllable), or *neumatic* (a mixture of the other two types). Melismas occur on accented syllables, important words, or penultimate syllables, and are often found setting such words as "Alleluia" or "Amen."

4. *Repeated notes*. In figures employing repeated white notes, each note carries a syllable.

5. *Imitation*. In imitative passages, each voice usually sets the text the same way.

[1]For exceptions, see the Appendix, p. 144, mm. 6, 8, 12, and 16.

6. The *final syllable* of the text falls on a strong beat, even if the syllable must immediately follow a series of quarters.

For those unfamiliar with Latin, translations are given after each work and each texted exercise, and accentuation is provided for the texts to be used in the exercises. Main accents are shown by the symbol ´ and secondary accents by the symbol.

Exercises

The following newly composed vocal lines contain various errors in text setting. Find the errors and explain why they are stylistically incorrect. The proper accentuation of the text is "Díes sanctificátus illúxit nóbis."

Notation and Performance Practice

The notation used in this text was chosen for its practicality. Those wishing more historical background may refer to the following sources, for which full bibliographic information is given in the Bibliography.

Apel, *The Notation of Polyphonic Music*;
The Harvard Dictionary of Music (2nd edition; refer to the following headings: Clef, Ligatures, Mensural Notation, Neumes, Notation, Notes, Partbooks, Partial Signatures, Proportions, Score, Staff, Tie, Time Signatures);
Jeppesen, *Counterpoint*, pp. 54–58.

In the musical examples in this text the half note is used as the unit of beat. Some modern performance editions employ the quarter note as the unit of beat. If such editions are used, it must be understood that all note values must be considered halved.

Most of the music used in this text was originally published in partbooks (each voice printed separately). The original notation lacked barlines (and therefore ties), complete text underlay, tempo, dynamic and phrasing indications. A feeling for the linearity, independence of voices, and rhythmic flexibility is greatly enhanced by performing from the original notation. A transcription into modern notation of the opening of the motet "Oculos in altum tollite" by Palestrina is given below. The **I** rest is worth four half-note beats.

Example 3

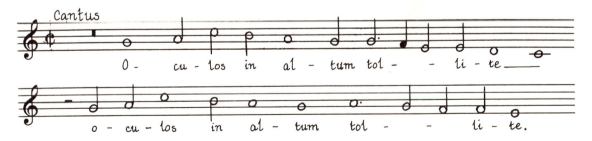

Translation: Lift up your eyes on high.

Exercises (Optional)

1. Perform the motet section above from the individual parts provided. Discuss the effect on the performance of singing from the parts, as distinct from singing from a score. What information relative to performance practice is missing from the parts? Read appropriate works on performance practice as suggested by the instructor and discuss the preparation of a proper historical performance of this work.

2. Discuss the problems of preparing a modern edition of the motet section above. How might a practical performance edition differ from a scholarly one, if at all? Prepare actual sample editions in score.

Rhythm and Meter

Sing again the motet *Dies sanctificatus*. Discuss the rhythm of each voice and the total rhythmic effect of the voices sung together. The following observations apply mainly to the sacred style and should not be assumed to be true of secular music of the time.

1. The music is metrical, but in a subtle way, song-dominated rather than dance-dominated. The effect of meter is achieved by placement of longer note values, suspensions, other dissonances, and cadences. Notes tending to sound accented are: high, long, cadential, approached by leap, syncopated, or those with syllabic stress. In general, accent in this music is more a matter of duration than of metric placement. The overall effect is fluid and undancelike.

2. To avoid excessively metrical effects, rhythmic symmetry is largely absent. Rhythmic sequence is rare, and periodic phrase structures are not found. Syncopation is common, as are dotted white-note values and ties into strong beats. Quarter notes tend to occur in odd-numbered groups. The effect of rests and ties (dotted values in the original notation), is to obscure the underlying meter.

3. The *meters* used in our transcriptions are $\frac{4}{2}$ ($\mathrm{\mathbb{C}}$) and $\frac{3}{1}$ (or $\frac{6}{2}$). Triple meters are much less common than duple and are rarely used for an entire work. The beat in triple meters is faster, so that white-note values predominate in triple-meter sections.[2] In $\frac{4}{2}$ meter, beats 1 and 3 are equally accented.

4. Each phrase tends to start slowly, gradually accelerate through the use of shorter notes, and slow at the cadence. The first voice enters on beat 1, and the cadence occurs on a strong beat. Long successions of any single note value are avoided, resulting in a variety of values in each phrase. Generally, the thicker the texture the longer the values, except where a climactic effect is desired.

---

[2]According to the system of metrical *proportions*, three beats in $\frac{3}{1}$ were equal in duration to one beat in $\frac{4}{2}$. In $\frac{3}{2}$, three beats were equal in duration to two beats in $\frac{4}{2}$.

5. The rhythm of each voice is known as the *microrhythm* and the combined rhythmic effect of all the voices together as the *macrorhythm* (see Jeppesen, *The Style of Palestrina and the Dissonance*, pp. 18–29). The effect of meter comes more from the macrorhythm than from the microrhythm. Note the subtle counterpointing of accents in the motet *Dies sanctificatus*, especially in measures 10ff. and 40ff.

6. *Note-values, rests, dots, and ties.* In the motet above, observe the use of the various note values, rests, and ties. Notice where each is placed in the measure, how each is preceded and followed, and how many of a given value are used in succession.

Note Values

There are six commonly used note values:

Example 4

Their use, to generalize, is as follows:

(1) The longa ⌐ is used only at the end of a section or complete work.
(2) The brevis ⊢ is used at the end, occasionally at the beginning.
(3) The semibrevis ○ is used like the brevis and is used within the phrase.
(4) The minima ♩ is the unit of beat and is the most common note value except in melismatic passages.

(5) The semiminima ♩ is a very common value. Semiminimas most often begin on the weak half of a beat and are often found in odd-numbered groups, in mid-phrase. Two semiminimas often replace one minima on a weak beat. It is unusual to find more than about nine semiminimas in succession in any voice.

(6) The fusa ♪ is very restricted in use. The typical idiom consists of two fusas in succession used as passing tones or in a lower-neighbor figure.

Triplet figures are extremely rare in this music; they are not to be used in writing.

Example 5

Rests

In this music there are three available rests:

brevis   semibrevis   minima

The first two types can begin only on strong beats.

Dots and Ties

As used in modern transcriptions:

(1) Any value other than ♩ or ♪ may be dotted.

(2) Ties are normally in a 1:1 or 2:1 note value ratio. The shorter note can be first only at the end of a work or section, as in ↄ|H‖³ Ties from quarters are very rare, so that the idiom | ♩♩♩|(=| ♩♩♩♩|) is highly unusual, especially in the sacred style. Ties to or from ♪ are not found.

(3) As a consequence of the above, a dotted semibrevis (𝅝.) may begin only on beats 1 or 3 (in quadruple meter), and a dotted minima (♩.) must start on the beginning of a beat.

---

³A rare exception may be found in the Appendix, p. 150, mm. 8-9.

(4) The tie into a strong beat is useful in avoiding too much strong-beat activity and too obvious a sense of meter.

(5) To check their feasibility, all dotted values should first be written out as ties. For example, $\vert \! \downarrow \ \text{o.} \vert$ is equal to $\vert \! \downarrow \! \downarrow \ \text{o} \vert$ and is therefore not to be used.

Exercises

Criticize the following melodic lines from the point of view of rhythm. Discuss both general stylistic aspects and technical specifics.

Harmony

Sing again the motet *Dies sanctificatus*. Discuss the harmony in general terms and consider such matters as: chord types (triad quality and inversion), harmonic rhythm, modulatory schemes, cadence placement and types, nonharmonic tones (types, metric placement, and note values involved), doubling, and use of accidentals. Find the chord roots on each beat and make a graph of them. Discuss the frequency of various types of root movement (by second, third, and so on, and whether up or down).

General Observations

MODULATION AND KEY SCHEME. In this style, one finds a degree of unification by key (mode and tonal center), but little evidence of the structural, form-building kinds of key schemes present in later music. The chordal vocabulary is well-defined, but chord placement has less effect on phrase and form than it does in the Baroque and later periods. Transposition of themes (except for imitative answers, usually on the dominant) is not employed in a systematic, formal way; indeed, one rarely sees both a natural mode and its transposition in the same work. Tonal variety is achieved not through modulation and transposition but through internal (medial) cadences on various degrees of a mode (see Modality below).[4] Chord is clearly subordinate to line, at least in contrapuntal passages. Composers of the period were aware not so much of chords as of combinations of harmonic intervals—not "major triad" but "major third with perfect fifth." Later composers often seem to begin with a harmonic scheme, on which the lines are superimposed. This is true of the music of this time only in certain variation and dance forms.

Root progressions are less predictable (i.e., patterned), and there is typically more root movement by seconds and thirds than in functional tonal music. The triads built on modal (scale) degrees two, three, and six are used more often than in later music. Functional formulae are concentrated around cadence

[4]Indeed, modulation in the tonal sense does not really exist here. There is, more accurately, oscillation between modal tonics.

points. In fact, it is at the cadence that one first begins to find clearly functional progressions and supportive bass lines. Roman numeral functional analysis is not really applicable here, except perhaps at cadences. The secular style, typically homophonic and progressive, is often more chordally conceived. Harmonic rhythm is usually slow, moving in whole- or half-note values, with a slowing of the harmonic rhythm at phrase endings.

Modality

Mode implies far more than scale. While "scale" may imply a convenient, abstract ordering of the main pitch material of a work, mode is "a sum of melodic or harmonic impulses . . . attaching to certain tones and . . . tending toward the principal tone."[5] Each mode features certain melodic idioms and emphasizes certain tones, certain accidentals (*ficta*), and especially its own cadential idioms. The modality of any work may not be clear until the final cadence. Moreover, modes are often freely mixed in a given work, so that modal theory and modal practice are not necessarily the same.

THE MODES.   The six modes, as found in the music of the late sixteenth century, are:

Example 6

$\text♩$ = *final (tonic)*
● = *usual harmonic and melodic dominant*
∨ = *half step*

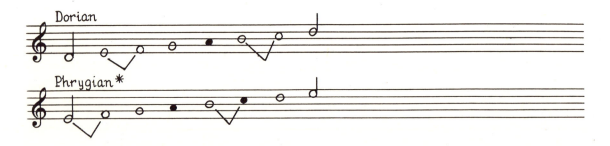

[5]Jeppesen, *Counterpoint*, p. 62.

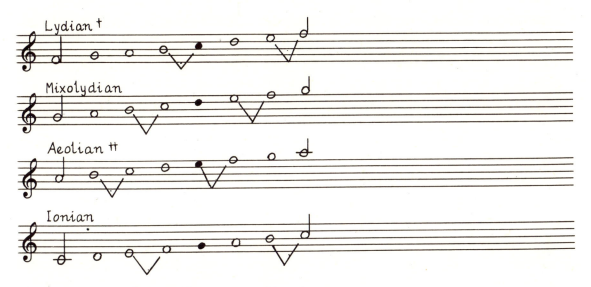

*B is the melodic dominant, but not a possible caden-
tial chord root. A and C are harmonic dominants, and
imitative entries often begin on A or C.

†Because of the universal use of B♭ in Lydian it becomes in effect the Ionian mode transposed up a perfect
fourth. The Lydian mode in its pure form will not be used
in this text.

††E is the melodic dominant, but cadences on D are
more common.

The distinction between authentic and plagal modes, while useful for the analysis of plainchant, is of no practical value here and will not be discussed.

The mode is expressed clearly at the end of a work, but often not at its beginning, although many pieces begin on tonic or dominant notes. Internal cadences may emphasize notes other than tonic and dominant (see Cadences, below).

By the end of the sixteenth century, the modes had begun to merge into the modern major and minor scales because of the use of *musica ficta* (see Accidentals, below). Dorian and Aeolian merged into minor; Mixolydian, Lydian, and Ionian merged into major. The Ionian mode is distinct from modern major only in the absence of clearly functional harmony, and because of the common use of B♭ in Ionian works.

Any mode can be transposed up a perfect fourth (or down a perfect fifth) by the use of B♭ as a signature or consistently used accidental. B♭ was the only commonly used signature at the time.

The final (tonic) and dominant notes are made clear by melodic emphasis and by their use in cadences. Note that all dominants are a fifth above the final, with the exception of the Phrygian mode.

The mode built on B (Locrian), while a theoretical possibility, was not used at the time because it lacks a perfect fifth above the final.

In the late sixteenth century, the modes were employed in the following descending order of frequency: Dorian, Ionian, Mixolydian, Aeolian, Phrygian. The last two modes were used relatively rarely.

Exercises

1. Memorize the names, finals, dominants, and half step placement of the untransposed modes. Which have minor triads built on the final? Which have major? Compare the intervallic structure of the Dorian, Phrygian, and Aeolian modes. Compare in the same way the Ionian, Lydian, and Mixolydian modes.

2. What is the final and the mode in each of the following examples from Lassus? How is the final emphasized? (Some examples have been transposed, using B♭; some are ambiguous as to final.)

e.

Accidentals (Musica Ficta)

The use of accidentals, either written in the music or as a signature (B♭ only) or as *musica ficta* is common at this time and signals the final decline of modality and the rise of major-minor tonality at the beginning of the seventeenth century.[6] The beginnings of functional tonality go far back historically, but tonality was not fully established until the end of the seventeenth century.

The only regularly used accidentals are B♭, E♭, F♯, C♯, and G♯.[7] B♭ is the most common and can be found even in plainchant. Accidentals are used:

(1) To avoid a melodic or harmonic tritone:

Example 7

B♭ rather than F♯ is normally used to correct the tritone from F to B.

(2) To avoid the augmented second between F and G♯ (Aeolian and Phrygian):

Example 8

[6]The practice of *musica ficta* involved the adding of accidentals by the performers, who improvised according to well-established melodic and harmonic procedures. In modern editions, editorial *ficta* are usually placed above the affected note. In writing the exercises, all accidentals should be specified.

[7]When a mode is transposed by the use of B♭ in the signature A♭ becomes available, but G♯ is not used.

(3) To raise the leading tone in cadences (Dorian, Aeolian, or Mixolydian):

Example 9

(4) To raise the third in the last chord in a strong cadence (Phrygian, Dorian, or Aeolian):

Example 10

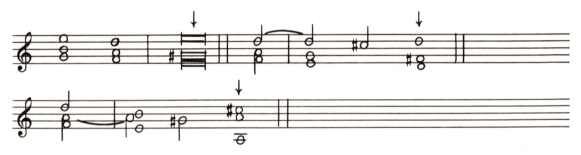

COMMENTS ON THE USE OF ACCIDENTALS.   B♭ is by far the accidental used most often in this music. It is preferred to F♯ to correct the tritone between F and B. All augmented or diminished melodic intervals are avoided or are corrected by appropriate *ficta*. B♭ is least common in the Phrygian and Aeolian modes.

The use of B♭ in the Lydian mode causes it to merge with the Ionian. The use of F♯ in Mixolydian has the same effect. If B♭ is used often in a work in Dorian, the effect is that of Aeolian transposed. The overuse of accidentals leads to the loss of individuality of mode; the practice should be avoided.

CROSS-RELATION. The close proximity of a note in its natural form to the same note altered is called cross-relation. This can occur within one voice, or between two voices:

Example 11

Cross-relation is an effect generally avoided in the conservative sacred style, although it is found occasionally in the works of English church composers such as Byrd and Gibbons.

Example 12

CHROMATICISM. Direct chromaticism is foreign to the Palestrina style and should be avoided in writing. A line will rarely contain two consecutive half-steps.

Exercises

1. What are the possible accidentals? In what ways are accidentals used in the style? Sing again the motet *Dies sanctificatus* and any other works of the period. Find all the accidentals and discuss their uses. Are there places where you think *musica ficta* might have been applied by singers of the time, or might have been inserted by the editor? Try singing the works again without accidentals and compare the results.

2. Discover the errors in the use of accidentals in the following examples and suggest possible corrections.

3. Add accidentals where appropriate:

Cadences

A cadence may emphasize any note except B (or any accidental) as the root of the final harmony in the cadence. The chart below gives for each mode the most common cadence notes (in line and harmony) in descending order of frequency:

Dorian	D A F
Phrygian	E A G
Lydian	F A C
Mixolydian	G D C
Aeolian	A D C
Ionian	C G A

Other cadential roots are possible in all the modes, but notice that cadences on E are common only in Phrygian and that cadences on B are not found.

Some of the most typical cadential idioms are given below, in a variety of textures and modes. The final chord always falls on a strong beat.

FINAL CADENCES

1. The authentic cadence (*clausula vera*), with implied or explicit dominant-to-tonic progression:

Example 13

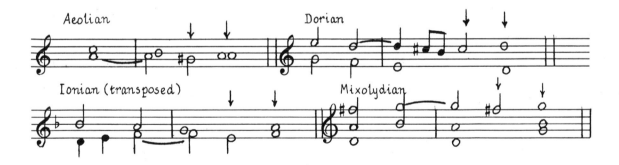

These idioms are common for all modes except Phrygian. Note that the leading tone is raised chromatically in authentic cadences on A, D, and G, that the final is usually suspended into the leading tone, that the upper voices usually approach the final by step from above and below, and that the final chord is in root position. If the final chord has a third, it is normally major. The final chord can be a tonic unison, a complete triad, or a triad without the third or without the fifth.

2. The Phrygian cadence (a type of authentic cadence):

Example 14

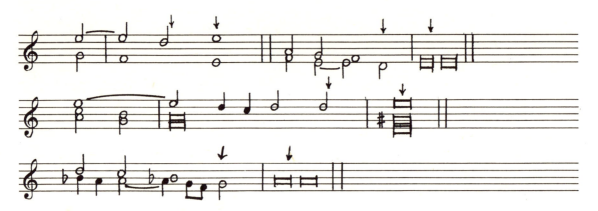

This cadence is characteristic of the Phrygian mode, though it may also occur on A, especially in the Dorian mode or (very rarely) on D. Note that the lower leading tone (D) is not raised and that the other voice descends a half step into the final.

3. The plagal cadence (the "Amen" cadence), with harmonies of subdominant or supertonic to tonic:

Example 15

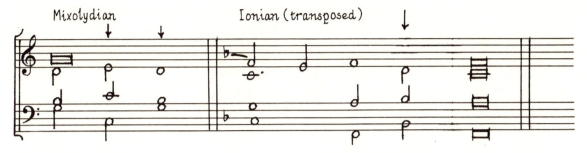

The plagal cadence is used in all modes, and is especially common in Aeolian and Phrygian. It is favored as a final cadence for an entire large section or complete work, often following an authentic or deceptive cadence.

INTERNAL (MEDIAL, PROGRESSIVE) CADENCES. Types (1) and (2) above are possible, in addition to:

4. The half (semi-) cadence, ending on dominant harmony:

Example 16

5. The deceptive cadence, with the progressions V-VI or V-IV, often in the context V-VI-IV-I (see example 17, below).[8]

Example 17

[8]The references to functional analysis are made here only for the convenience of those familiar with that system. It is generally inappropriate as an analytical tool for this music.

Exercises

1. In the motet *Dies sanctificatus* and in works selected by the instructor from the Appendix, find all the cadences, and discuss the mode, cadence type, voice movement into cadence, and motion over cadence, if any, in this music. Note the relation of each cadence final to the final of the whole work and plot out graphically their placement within the work, using a time-line graph such as the following:

Cadence final:	G	G	C	G	G
Measure:	7	10	14	20	25
Cadence type:	authentic	authentic	authentic	half	plagal

2. Identify mode and cadence type in the following Excerpts.

Chords

Even though the concepts of triad-identity and chord roots were not yet established by theory, composers of the period were clearly aware of the existence of certain pleasant-sounding vertical combinations. These were rarely used as the main focus of the music, except in homophonic passages, but resulted from the combination of moving voices.

The *harmonic intervals* used in the style can be grouped as shown in the chart below. The compounds of these intervals (the interval plus an octave) have the same degree of consonance or dissonance. In the chart, P stands for perfect intervals, M for major intervals, and m for minor.

CONSONANCES (STABLE, RELAXED)
M3, m3
P1, P5, P8
M6, m6

DISSONANCES (UNSTABLE, TENSE)
P4 (except as noted later)
All seconds and sevenths
All augmented (A) and diminished (d) intervals

CONSONANT CHORDS.   Above a given note, thirds, sixths, perfect fifths, and octaves are considered consonant.[9] Root position and first-inversion major and minor triads make up most of the vertical sonorities.

DISSONANT CHORDS.   Diminished triads in first inversion may be found; in root position they occur only under special conditions (see page 94).[10] Augmented triads are possible, but rarely, and only in first inversion. Seventh

---

[9]The thirds and sixths are called "imperfect" consonances, the fifths and octaves "perfect" consonances.

[10]Since both intervals above the lowest note (M6, m3) are consonant, the dissonance between the upper voices (A4 or d5) was considered acceptable. In general, the critical intervals, and those most carefully treated if dissonant, are those between the lowest voice and each of the upper voices.

chord effects are not considered consonant, and such effects rise out of nonharmonic activity.

The only chords commonly containing *accidentals* are:

Example 18

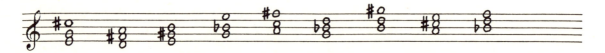

The B-minor triad (requiring an F♯) is not common. Triads in second inversion are considered dissonant because of the perfect fourth, and occur only under special conditions (see page 96).

DOUBLING.   Any note in a chord may be doubled except the leading tone in a cadence or the raised third in the final chord. Doubling of any accidental except B♭ is rare.

All *dissonances* are treated with the utmost care. The regulation of dissonance is more painstaking in this style than in any other style. Thus, the few allowable dissonances are all the more striking and expressive, especially those falling on strong beats. The only allowable nonharmonic tones are passing tones, auxiliaries, anticipations, the cambiata figure, and suspensions. The escape tone and appoggiatura are utterly foreign to the style. These dissonances are taken up in detail in Chapter 2.

Exercises

1. Look again at the motet *Dies sanctificatus*. Find all the dissonant notes and label them according to the type of nonharmonic tone usage they represent. First examine the harmonic vocabulary and make a list of the chords used in terms of chord root and type (quality), position, and doubling.

2. Label the chords and intervals below according to whether they are consonant or dissonant. Measure all chordal intervals from the lowest tone to each of the upper voices in turn.

Melody

Sing again the motet on p. 1 and any works from the Appendix suggested by the instructor. Sing the voices individually. Discuss the nature of the melodic lines. Some style characteristics to consider are:

The overall melodic contour (shape) of each phrase;

The vocality of the line;

The voice-ranges and the use of the extremes and the middle of each range;

Any distinctions between the function, character, or degree of activity of the different voices;

The presence or absence of any idioms or effects particularly associated with instrumental music or with more dramatic music;

The presence of periodic phrase structures, if any;

The presence of climax (where and how achieved);

The opening of each voice, in terms of note values, metrical placement, and direction;

The presence or absence of sequences;

The rhythmic shape of each phrase (increase and decrease of activity);

Any characteristic, recurrent melodic idioms or patterns;

The placement, types, and idioms of cadences;

The use of accidentals;

The modality of each voice, including shifts of mode;

The treatment of all leaps (in what note values, whether up or down, where placed metrically, how preceded and followed in the line);

The melodic intervals used (list according to their frequency, both ascending and descending).

General Observations

The bywords for melodic construction in this style are balance, flow, and restraint. Each line has a clear contour, often roughly in this form: ⌒ The high point is often placed around the middle of each phrase. One rarely finds such contours as ⌣, which is common in more dramatic music. Each phrase tends to rise slowly to one climactic point and to descend gradually to a cadence. The cadential gesture is normally a falling one. All sudden effects are avoided—there are no obtrusive or nervous rhythmic idioms—and lines do not begin or end abruptly. No single voice is much more active or interesting than any other. Extensive note-repetition is avoided, as are all idioms tending to create flat or aimless lines. The rhythm is that of prose rather than of metrical poetry, although it is superimposed on a subtly metrical framework. Each voice begins slowly and gathers speed gradually toward the climax of the phrase. The climactic note is often longer than the notes around it, and it is typically a tied or dotted value. The kinds of climactic effects found in later or more dramatic music (i.e., the large leap into a high, sustained note, especially an appoggiatura) are foreign to the style.

Largely missing here are long sequences (rhythmic or melodic), chromaticism, instrumental idioms (many successive skips, large range, complex ornaments, many fast notes), large or difficult intervals, dancelike rhythms and periodic phrase structures.

Refer again to the chart of voice-ranges on page 8. The extremes of each range are rarely used in a sustained passage. The heart or middle of each range (the *tessitura*) is emphasized. Rests are calculated to allow each singer time to breathe.

Intervals and Treatment of Leaps

This music is predominantly conjunct (stepwise). Leaps are treated with great caution (see below). The melodic intervals used are:

M2, m2
M3, m3
P4
P5
m6 (ascending only)
P8 (rare)

With few exceptions, major sixths, sevenths, and compound intervals (those greater than an octave) are not found. The following are some general observations concerning the treatment of leaps.

1. The larger intervals tend to occur with the slower note values; the faster the motion, the more the tendency to move conjunctly.

Example 19

Example 20

2. Leaps are most often approached and followed by motion in the opposite direction, for balance. Successive leaps occur most typically in white notes, forming triadic outlines.

Example 21

3. In ascending motion, the larger intervals usually come first; in descending, the smaller first. This is especially true in quarter-notes. In other words, the larger skips are most often *below* the smaller.

Example 22

4. Successive leaps in opposite directions are possible, but should not be overused.

Example 23

5. Aside from triadic outlines, successive leaps in one direction (especially in white notes) may also form the following intervallic successions: P5 + P4, P5 + m3, or more rarely P4 + P4. These idioms are more common in the bass voice than in the other voices.

Example 24

6. Ascending leaps are more carefully balanced than descending, as they are more obtrusive.

Example 25

7. The larger the leap, the stronger the tendency toward balancing the motion afterwards, by skip or by step.

Example 26

8. Leaps up to unaccented long notes, especially long notes that are tied or dotted, are common; leaps up to accented notes are less common.

Example 27

Exercises

1. Sing and discuss music from the Appendix suggested by the instructor. Pay particular attention to the treatment of leaps and compare to the comments above, keeping in mind that the comments are generalizations, not hard-and-fast rules.

2. In the following fragments, find the errors of style, technique, or musicality, and suggest simple ways of correcting them.

Other Aspects of Melody

1. Note repetition is typical only in homophonic sections, where it usually occurs in white notes and rarely for more than five repetitions. In white notes, each repetition carries a syllable of the text. In black notes, the only repetition is the anticipation figure.

Example 28

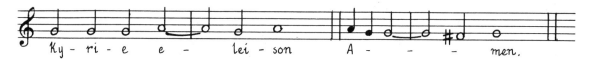

Ky – ri – e   e – lei – son   A – – – men.

2. Eighth notes are used in a very restricted way. They occur typically as stepwise-related pairs, on the weak part of a beat, after a quarter note or dotted half note. They may be passing tones, usually descending, or they may form a lower-auxiliary figure, especially to ornament the resolution of a suspension. They are ornamental in character, and either or both may be dissonant against the other voices. These pairs are rarely used in the same voice in close succession. Other eighth-note idioms, though possible, are extremely rare.

Example 29

3. The suspension figure is very common. It occurs most often in half notes, and its resolution may be ornamented in the following ways, among others. The suspension figure can, of course, occur even when the suspended note is not a dissonance. The suspension will be considered in detail in Chapter 2.

Example 30

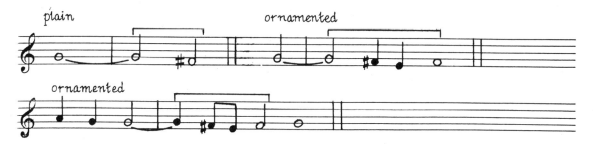

4. The cambiata figure is common in music of this period. The second note of the figure may be dissonant; it is the only dissonance left by leap in this style. The figure may start on any beat. Its inversion is possible, but only common in white note values, and the second note of the figure is then consonant. Typical versions are:

Example 31

(inversion)

5. The melodic cadential figures in this style are highly standardized.[11] In all authentic cadences the final is approached by step from above or below in at least one voice. The leading tone is raised chromatically as needed (Dorian, Mixolydian, Aeolian), and the suspension figure is almost obligatory as a preparation for it. In textures of three or more voices, the lowest voice may leap a fourth or fifth at the cadence. Cadences on B are not found; cadences on E are found most often in Phrygian, on F mainly in Dorian and Lydian. An authentic cadence on any note other than B or E is possible, as are Phrygian cadences on E, A, or (rarely) D.

Example 32

[11]Review Cadences, above.

6. The leading tone is usually approached by step, and most often from above. It often forms the resolution of a suspension figure. Composers (except for the English) generally avoid the proximity of subtonic and leading tone as this will cause a cross-relation.

Example 33

7. Review Comments on the Use of Accidentals above. The most used accidental is B♭ (though not in Phrygian). E♭, rarely used, occurs most often in Dorian. B♭ and E♭ are used principally to avoid tritone effects in the line; sharps are used principally in cadences. All chromaticisms and cross-relations are to be avoided at this stage in writing music in this style.

Any line emphasizing both F and B (by means of proximity, placement on strong beats, length of notes, or the use of one of these notes as the outer limit of a scalar figure), will normally require a B♭ to correct the tritone.

Example 34

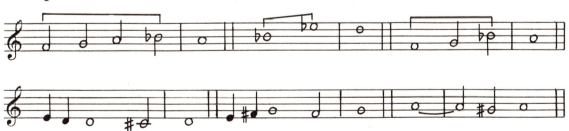

8. Brief sequences—more common in the music of Lassus than of Palestrina—are possible, but they should not be overused or extended beyond the third repetition of the sequential pattern.

Exercises

1. Sing and discuss the melodic lines found in polyphonic music assigned by the instructor. Discuss note repetition, the use of eighth notes, suspensions, cambiatas, cadential figures, and the reasons for accidentals.

2. Find the specific technical or stylistic errors in the following examples and suggest ways of correcting them.

Typical Quarter-note Idioms

Examine again the motet *Dies sanctificatus*, as well as the motets given in the Appendix, and discuss the use of quarter notes in the line. How are single quarter notes used? Note their approach, resolution, and placement in the measure. Look at quarter-note pairs similarly. What is the maximum number of quarters in succession? How are leaps treated? (How are they followed? Where are they placed metrically? In what direction do they go? What intervals are used?) What seem to be the typical idioms? What quarter-note figures typical of later styles are not found here?

The melodic treatment of quarter notes is very circumscribed and calls for special commentary.

1. Single quarter-note figures are the neighbor (auxiliary), most often a lower neighbor, the passing tone, and the anticipation (used as part of a suspension). The single quarter note is occasionally treated by skip, especially by Lassus (see page 51, measures 13-14).

Example 35

2. Pairs of quarter notes are most often treated stepwise, usually on a weak beat, following a whole note or a half note. When placed on a strong beat, the second note is usually an anticipation.

Example 36

3. Series of quarters rarely exceed eight or nine notes. Squareness can be avoided by using an uneven number of quarters in a series. They are usually left by step, or by leap in the opposite direction to a white note.

Example 37

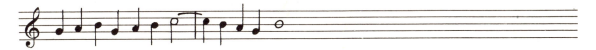

4. Ascending leaps from accented quarters are very rare, as are ascending leaps from dotted half notes.

Example 38

5. Since skipping figures returning to the first note sound aimless and "fussy," they are avoided, especially where the middle note of the figure is above the other notes.

Example 39

6. Leaps are normally balanced by motion in the opposite direction. Large leaps are rare.

Example 40

7. Successive leaps in quarters are so rare in the sacred style as to be considered unusable.

Example 41

8. Pentatonic figures are very rare. It is in this aspect that line in this music differs most from plainchant.

Example 42

9. Sequences, rare in any note values, are especially unusual in quarter notes.

Exercises

Sing or play the following lines and discuss the problems in the use of quarter notes. Some lines merely contain idioms unusual for the style, while others obviously contain errors of technique.

Cumulative Exercises for Melody

1. Sing and study plainchant. Some chants are given on pages 133-135 of the Appendix. In what ways are these similar to the type of line you have been studying? In what ways are they different? Consider all aspects, general as well as specific. This exercise is optional.

2. Study the following melodies, all fragments of Kyrie settings. Compare them in terms of text setting, general style, and technical specifics.

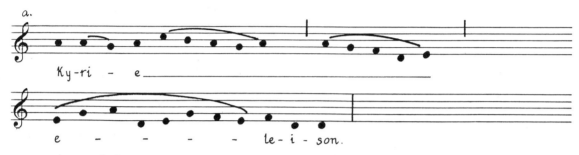

a.

Ky-ri - e _____ e - - - - le - i - son.

Kyrie from Mass IV (*Liber Usualis*, p. 25)

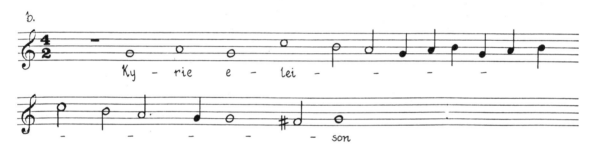

b.

Ky - rie e - lei - - - - - - son

Palestrina, Kyrie from *Missa ad Fugam* (superius, mm. 1-6)

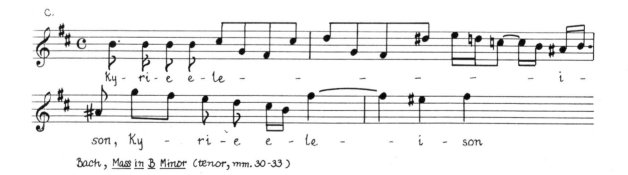

c.

Ky - ri - e e - le - - - - - i -
son, Ky - ri - e e - le - - i - son

Bach, *Mass in B Minor* (tenor, mm. 30-33)

3. Criticize the following "melody" in general (stylistic and musical) and specific (technical) terms. If simple solutions to technical errors are possible, suggest them.

4. Compose melodies in the Palestrina style, based on the following rhythmic patterns. Use vocal ranges and untransposed modes as suggested by the instructor. One of these might be composed together in class. Sing and discuss all work before going on to the next exercises.

a.

b.

c.

5. Compose melodies of three to four measures in each mode, for a variety of voice-ranges, ending in an authentic cadence. Use only the standard cadential melodic figures.

6. Compose melodies in the style for soprano, alto, or tenor vocal ranges in a variety of untransposed modes. Think of these as one voice of a polyphonic texture, but make them independent and self-contained, with no long internal rests. Use $\frac{4}{2}$ meter and barlines (optional). Write several melodies without text, eight to twenty measures long. Sing and discuss these in class, making whatever corrections are needed before setting the texts given below, as assigned by the instructor. Accentuation is added.

(a) Bènedíctus qui veńit/in nómine Dómini
(b) Qui tóllis peccáta múndi
(c) Chríste eléison (set as e-lei-son or e-le-i-son)
(d) Allelúia
(e) Amén

While composing these lines, keep the following points in mind:

a. Some use of text repetition is appropriate. Study text repetition in the works you have sung.

b. Begin on a strong beat, on the tonic or dominant.

c. Start with longer note values and gradually introduce shorter notes.

d. Work for a balance of steps and leaps, a clear overall contour, a clear and well-placed climax, and a smooth descent to a standard cadential idiom on a strong beat.

e. Avoid squareness by using dots, ties (suspensions), and short rests. Use a variety of note values in each phrase.

f. Avoid extended sequences.

g. Use only the available intervals, and be particularly careful of lines emphasizing the tritone.

h. Watch carefully the treatment of all leaps and all black notes.

i. Use normal voice ranges, and avoid the extremes of each range.

j. Try to work away from the piano, and sing all your work.

k. Remember that this is *expressive* music, but not in any way abrupt or overtly dramatic. Work for smoothness and fluidity.

All writing should be sung and discussed in class. Multiple copies, an overhead projector, or work on a lined blackboard will facilitate both performance and discussion.

Two-voice Counterpoint Chapter 2

SING BOTH of the two-voice motets below, focusing on the relationships between the voices. Discuss the two motets in terms of the following:

1. What is the rhythmic relationship between the voices? Is one voice more active than the other? How often do they move at the same time, in the same note values? Are there any beats on which neither voice is moving? Is there any overall change in activity within the phrase? Is the meter clear, and how is it emphasized or obscured? Write out the rhythmic structure as follows:

Oculus non vidit:

2. Examine phrase and contour. Is there a clear sense of phrase? Do the voices end and/or begin their phrases together? How are phrase endings obscured or overlapped? How long are the phrases? What different modal degrees are used as cadence finals? Are the phrases regular, balanced, periodic? Generalize about the overall form of a motet. Is "form" an accurate word here?

3. How are the voices organized motivically (thematically)? Is there imitation? Are there any clearly unifying motives? Is there any use of inversion, augmentation, or diminution of motives? If there is imitation, explore the metrical and pitch intervals between the voices where the imitation begins. For how long is the imitation strict?

4. Discuss the cadences in terms of intervals between the voices, dissonance treatment, melodic idioms, mode, final, use of accidentals, and types and strengths of cadences.

5. Label the intervals formed between the two voices on every beat and, where there is quarter-note activity, the intervals formed off the beat. What intervals are present? Which ones predominate? Where are the various intervals found metrically? What kinds of note values are involved? Especially note the dissonant intervals (seconds, fourths, sevenths, and so on); how are they treated in terms of metrical placement, note values involved, melodic approach and resolution?

6. Discuss the relative motion (parallel, contrary, similar, oblique) from beat to beat. Does any one type predominate? What kinds of parallel intervals are used, and what kinds are not used?

7. How is the text set? Consider the overall atmosphere or mood of the text and its setting, the means of emphasis (important words and stressed syllables), and the relation, if any, between text form and musical form.

Example 43

BEATUS HOMO   *Lassus*

Blessed is the man that findeth wisdom and is rich in prudence: the purchasing thereof is better than the merchandise of silver, and the chiefest and purest gold.

Example 44

Lassus

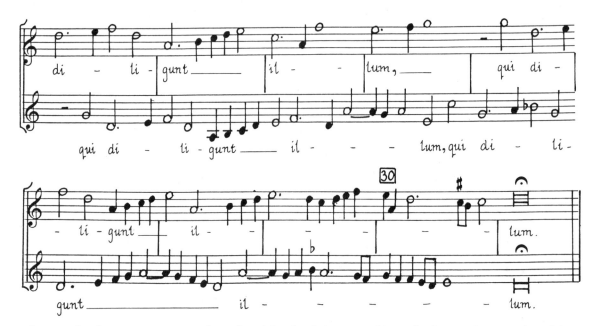

That eye hath not seen, nor ear heard, neither hath it entered into the heart of man, what things God hath prepared for them that love Him.

General Observations

Counterpoint, which implies line-against-line, not point-against-point, involves two or more voices moving and interrelating in a somewhat independent way. No music with more than one voice is entirely without contrapuntal aspects, and some music that is often studied for its "harmonic" content is in fact more linearly than harmonically conceived. The Baroque chorale style, for example, is distinctly contrapuntal in nature, not simply one chord after the next. Late sixteenth-century sacred vocal style is typified by a texture in which the voices move with a high degree of independence, regulated mainly by a few simple procedures of dissonance control. Each voice is satisfying in itself as an expressive vocal line, and is not merely the linearization of a preconceived harmonic background.

Rhythm

The voices are equally active, especially when imitative. The basic unit of movement is the half note, with an increase of movement through each phrase and a slowing at the cadence. There is activity on each beat in at least one voice, except sometimes at the beginning or end of the phrase. The voices often move in different note values, and passages of simultaneous motion (homophony) are usually short. The meter is expressed mainly through dissonance placement and cadences and is subtly obscured through the use of ties, dotted values, strong-beat rests, the placement of whole notes starting on beats two or four, and suspensions.

Texture

Two-voice counterpoint in this style is usually imitative, tending less to the homophonic (familiar) style than does music with three or more voices. Short homophonic passages are used for relief of the prevailingly imitative texture. Close spacing is the norm, with the voices rarely more than a tenth apart. Voice-crossing is not carried on for long passages.

Phrase and Form

Each section that sets a new part of the text tends to begin imitatively and to end in a cadence. An excessively cadential effect is avoided by dropping out one voice momentarily at cadence points and bringing it back immediately with a new theme, allowing the voices to cadence at different times. Alternatively, one voice may be held over past the cadence point and elided into the next phrase.

Example 45

Lassus

Example 46

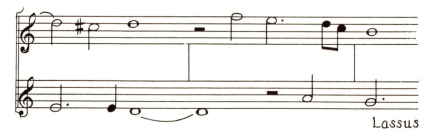

Lassus

Cadential idioms are discussed below. Periodic effects are of course avoided. A two-voice motet or mass-section in the imitative style is built up formally of a series of points-of-imitation (subsections, each setting a new part of the text and ending with a cadence). The last section often displays the most rhythmic activity, the most melismatic setting, and tends to sound the most climactic.

Motivic (Thematic) Organization

This music lacks the clear kinds of motivic unity and developmental processes associated with later music. At the same time, a subtle kind of unification by interval (or figure or "cell") often does occur, or a work may be unified by an underlying plainchant theme. Each phrase, though, may be thought of as to some degree independent and self-contained. The systematic use of strict canon, thematic inversion, augmentation, or diminution as large-scale structural devices is less common than in earlier Netherlandish music, with the exception of a few special works such as the *Missa Ad fugam* of Palestrina.

Technical Details

Motion Relationships

There is normally a good mixture of motion types (parallel, similar, contrary, oblique) between the voices. No one type should be allowed to predominate. Both voices will rarely leap simultaneously in the same direction, and in such cases, neither will leap more than a perfect fourth.

o = *oblique*   p = *parallel*
s = *similar*   c = *contrary*

Example 47

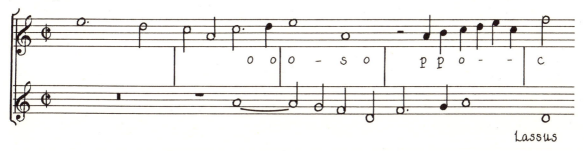

Lassus

The only real restrictions on relative motion concern *parallel* intervals.

1. Parallel thirds and sixths are allowed, but a series of more than about five tends to obscure the independence of the voices and is usually reserved for quarter-note motion in melismatic passages. The following idiom, successive major thirds, is best avoided unless the tritone can be resolved.

Example 48

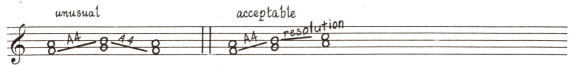

2. Parallel seconds and sevenths may be considered unusable.

3 Parallel fourths, common only in three-voice texture, are found there in series of parallel first-inversion triads.

Example 49

4. Parallel fifths, octaves, and unisons are not found, but the following points should be noted.

    a. Near-parallel fifths are occasionally found in the following idiom, rationalized by the fact that the voices do not move simultaneously. This idiom is rarely found between the outer voices of a many-voiced texture, and does not apply to parallel octaves.

Example 50

    b. Parallel fifths or octaves are not normally found on successive beats or on successive *strong* beats, even if consonant notes intervene.

Example 51

    c. Fifths and octaves by contrary motion are found in music with more than two voices, though rarely between the outer voices. They are best avoided in two-voice writing.

Example 52

    d. Unequal fifths (perfect to diminished or the reverse) are not normally found in two voices. They occur in thicker textures, but not between the outer voices.

Example 53

    e. Direct (covered) octaves and fifths are rarely found in two-voice counterpoint, and then only when the upper voice moves by step. They may be found in thicker textures, but not usually between outer voices.

Example 54

    f. Movement by leap into a unison is not used, even when achieved by contrary motion.

Example 55

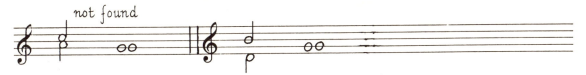

Intervallic Relationships

CONSONANCES. The freely used harmonic intervals, as we have seen, are the thirds, the perfect fifth, the sixths, the unison, the octave and their compounds. Two-voice counterpoint tends toward a preponderance of thirds, sixths, and fifths on the beat. Unisons are typical only at cadences or as short weak-beat notes. Too many unisons, octaves, and fifths weaken the harmonic tension. The final interval is normally a tonic unison or an octave approached by step in contrary motion. Voices moving simultaneously in the same note values are usually consonant with each other. Unison or octave doubling of any scale degree is possible, except of any accidental, especially the leading tone. Whole notes are always consonant, except for an occasional long suspension at a final cadence.

DISSONANCES.   The treatment of dissonance is an important aspect of the study of counterpoint. There was considerable agreement among composers of the time as to the allowable types of dissonances, their introduction, resolution, and placement in the measure. In general, one never leaps to or from a dissonance, with the exception of the cambiata figure. Only values shorter than the brevis (⊟) or the semibrevis (o) can normally be dissonant. The passing tone and suspension are the most common dissonances. In two-voice writing, no note longer than a quarter can be dissonant against notes of equal value. Dissonance occurs only in the idioms described below.

1. Auxiliary (neighbor) notes, in ♩ and ♪ only, fall only on the weak part of a beat, and are much more typically lower than upper neighbors. The upper auxiliary figure is usually consonant.

Example 56

2. Passing tones in ♩ fall on weak beats only, usually descending. They rarely follow ♩ activity, and never a ♩ passing tone.

Example 57

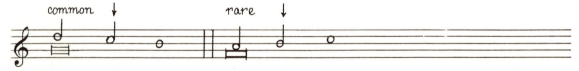

Passing tones in ♩ fall on the weak part of any beat, ascending or descending, and on the beginning of beats two or four, descending only. The latter are less common.

Example 58

Note in the following example that the passing ♪ following a tied or dotted ♩ is a common idiom (see a); that the accented passing tone is most often the first of a pair of ♪ (see b); that two successive ♪ may both be dissonant, if both are treated normally (see c); and that unaccented ♪ may be dissonant against each other, if the dissonance is treated normally (see d).

Example 59

Two passing ♪ may replace a passing ♪ on the weak half of a beat.

Example 60

3. Anticipations (*portamenti*), in ♪ only, fall on the weak part of any beat. When approached from below, they are consonant; when approached from above they may be either dissonant or not. They are most typically found in the following cadential idioms:

Example 61

4. Review the cambiata figure on page 38. The second note of the cambiata figure is the only dissonance left by leap. The first and third notes are consonant; the fourth note may be consonant or a passing tone. The first note is never treated as a suspension.

Example 62

5. The suspension, the only strong-beat dissonance in this music, is a major expressive device. The suspension idiom involves consonant preparation, dissonance on the same pitch on a strong beat, and resolution down by step to a consonance.[13] The dissonant note is a half note, but may be ornamented before resolution. The preparation is a half or whole note, and is in no case shorter than the suspension. The preparation and suspension need not be tied if the suspension carries a different syllable. Melodic figures associated with the suspension may also occur when no dissonance is involved. Some typical suspension idioms follow:

Example 63

P = Preparation   S = Suspension   R = Resolution

[13]But see the comments on triple meter, p. 62.

Note in the example above some typical ornamentations of the resolution (shown in b, c, e and f); that the consonant voice often has two successive quarter notes, the first of which is an accented passing tone on beat two or four, the second of which forms a unison or octave with the preparation (shown in b and e); that a consonant anticipation often precedes the preparation note (see c and e); that a cadential suspension always involves the final resolving to the leading tone or (in Phrygian) subtonic; that the consonant voice may move simultaneously with the resolution (see d); and that at the end of a work a suspension in whole notes is possible (see f).

Suspensions are often classified in terms of the intervals formed between the two voices on the dissonant and resolution parts of the figure. The only suspensions typical of two-voice texture are the 7–6, 2–3 (suspension in the lower voice), and, rarely, the 4–3. The 6–5 suspension, while possible, is not very effective, since the sixth is not dissonant. In the 4–3 suspension, the fourth is almost always perfect. 9–8, 2–1 and 4–3 suspensions are common in textures with more voices.

Example 64

Occasionally, in a series of parallel thirds descending stepwise in half notes, one note will be delayed a half beat, causing what seems to be a suspension in quarter notes. This is not a true suspension but merely a rhythmic variant.

Example 65

6. Some characteristic dissonance treatments in triple meter ($_2^6$) are given below. Note that in all cases the dissonant voice moves in quicker note values than the other voice. Passing tones in half notes can occur on the even beats (2, 4, 6), and passing tones in quarters can occur off the beat or descending on even beats. In suspension figures, the dissonance is located on beats one or five. Cadences may occur on any odd beat internally, but only on beat one at the end.

Example 66

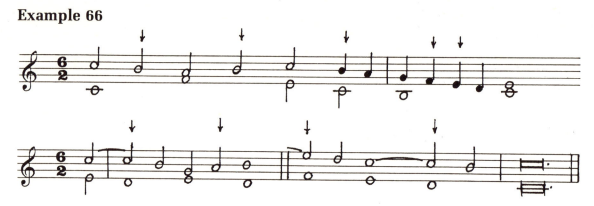

In $_2^3$ meter (the half note as the beat), half notes are all consonant, and only smaller values may be dissonant.

Cadential Idioms

Review the material on cadences and suspensions above. Cadential figuration is very standardized in this style, as we have seen. Below are some of the most popular idioms, shown in a variety of modes.

Example 67

Comments on Two-voice Composition

The following suggestions should be kept in mind while working out the exercises below.

1. Sing all your work as you write it. Try to work away from the piano and use it only for checking. Better yet, check your work with voices or single-line instruments.

2. Use only the untransposed modes and the usual accidentals (sparingly). For now, work only in $\frac{4}{2}$. Avoid cross-relations.

3. Remember that you are writing *music,* not theory exercises. The result should be as musical (vocal, flowing, expressive) as possible. Sing each line through as you write it, and never choose a note on a purely vertical (harmonic) basis. Avoid squareness of phrase, too many successive equal note values, and too much simultaneous movement in both voices. Do not accept flat or aimless lines. Ties and short rests can be effective in promoting a fluid result, as can the placement of whole notes starting on beat two. When one voice is static, the other should be relatively active. Avoid strong-beat unisons or octaves except at phrase endings. Extended passages of wide spacing should not be used.

4. Some of the following exercises can be written and checked during class. The most extended compositional ones obviously cannot. All student exercises and compositions should be sung in class and criticized by the students. Time permitting, they should be corrected together at the blackboard. The voices should be sung individually, then together.

Exercises

No imitation is required in this written work.

1. Sing as many two-voice works in the style as possible and analyze them in terms of stylistic and technical details. The best single source is the *Can-*

tiones duarum vocum from the *Magnum Opus* of Orlandus Lassus (see the Appendix, pages 135-144).

2. Prepare a systematic summary of the placement, duration, and treatment (preparation and resolution) of all dissonances, perhaps using the following sample format:

Type	Note Values	Metric Placement	Treatment
Anticipation	Quarter	Off the beat	Approached by step, resolved on the same pitch

3. Find the errors of style or technique in the following "composition." These may affect line or counterpoint. Discuss ways in which they could be corrected. Pay particular attention to all dissonances.

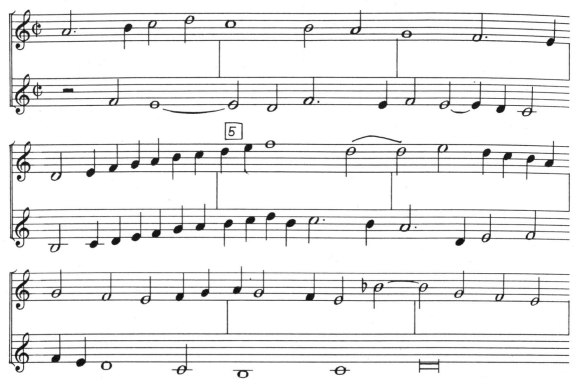

4. Write two- to three-measure examples, for two adjacent voices (S-A, A-T, or T-B), of the following idioms:

(a) Passing tones in half notes;
(b) Passing tones in quarter notes and eighth notes;
(c) Auxiliaries (neighbors);
(d) Consonant and dissonant anticipations;
(e) The cambiata figure;
(f) 7–6, 2–3, and 4–3 suspensions, with and without ornamentation.

Use a fairly simple texture, ¢ meter, and a variety of modes. These should be done carefully and neatly, as they are intended to serve as useful reference examples for dissonance treatment and other idioms.

5. To each of the lines given below, add a second voice

(a) mainly in half notes, some of which may be suspended (a few quarters may be used);

(b) mainly in quarter notes, with a few half and eighth notes used for smoothness of line and rhythmic variety.

To each given line, add a voice above, then a different voice below. Each voice should cadence at the end. These will naturally be rhythmically dull, but should still be as musical as possible. The primary purpose of this exercise is to gain control of dissonance and to see the contrapuntal possibilities inherent in a given musical line. Start on a unison, or an octave or fifth away from the given line. You may begin with a one-beat rest. Use dissonances where appropriate. End on a unison or octave. It is recommended that some of these be done in class at the blackboard.

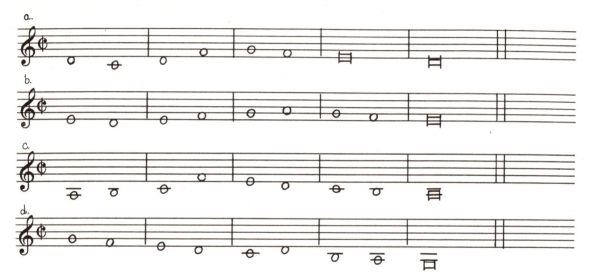

It is suggested that you

    (a) Write each voice on a separate staff;
    (b) Avoid extended voice crossing or many compound intervals;
    (c) Do not overuse parallel motion;
    (d) Analyze all dissonances and check for correctness in the style.

6. After the preliminary exercises above have been completed, sung, and corrected in class, proceed to add new voices in mixed note values above and below the given lines. Any of the given lines may now be transposed up a

fourth or down a fifth, for ease of singing. These new melodies should be as stylistically and technically correct as possible.

7. Now add new voices, first above and then below the original melodies composed in Exercise 6.

8. Add new voices in mixed note values above and then below the given lines in the following cadential measures. End on a unison or octave.

9. Compose three to four measures in two voices, in all modes, each ending with standard authentic cadential formulae.

10. Add new voices, first above and then below the following given voices. Imitation is not required. The given voice may be treated as soprano or tenor. The new voice should also set the text. One of these might be done together in class.

Translation: *Christ have mercy on us.*

Translation: *I will praise the name of the Lord.*

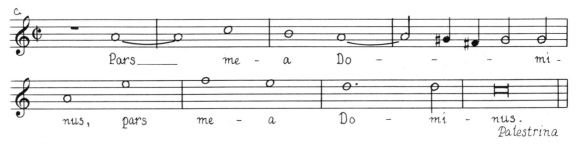

Translation: *The Lord is my portion.*

11. Continue the motet openings given below for eight to twelve more measures, ending in a strong authentic cadence. If you wish at this point to experiment with imitation, study pages 70-76, but no further imitation is required in these pieces. All are taken from the *Cantiones duarum vocum*.

Imitation in Two-voice Texture

Sing the Lassus motet openings below (Examples 68–74). Discuss the imitation found in them in terms of:

(1) The time-distance, in beats, between entrances;

(2) The pitch interval between the first notes of the two voices (called leader and follower) and the modal degree on which each begins;

(3) The length of imitation (the number of beats during which the second voice imitates the first);

(4) Whether the response (the following voice) is real or tonal (see General Observations below for a definition of real and tonal imitation);

(5) Any special features, such as stretto (see below) or imitation by augmentation, diminution, or inversion.

Example 68

Translation: The righteous man commits his heart to watching at the break of day.

Example 69

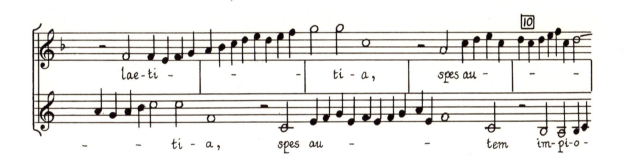

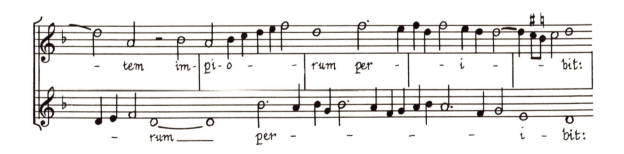

Translation: The expectation of the just is joy, but the hope of the unrighteous shall perish.

Example 70

Translation: Who follows me. . . . (Note the text-painting.)

Example 71

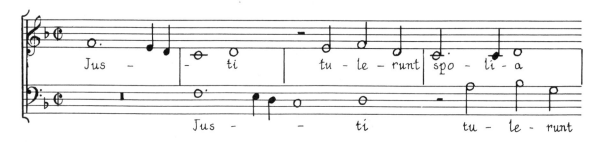

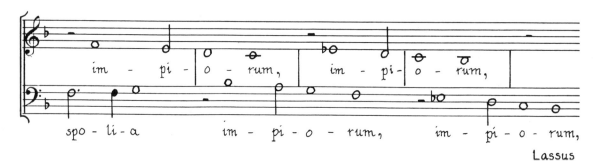

Translation: The just have taken up the spoils of the unrighteous.

Example 72

Ser - ve bo - ne et fi de - - - - lis

Ser - ve bo - ne et fi - de - lis

Translation: *Good and faithful servant . . .*

Example 73

Qui vult ve-ni - re post me, ve-ni - re post me, ve-

Qui vult ve-ni - re post me, ve-ni - re post me, ve-ni -

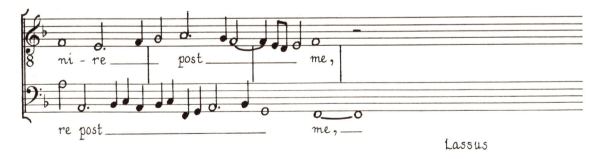

ni - re post me,

re post me,

Lassus

Translation: *Who wishes to follow me . . .*

Example 74

Translation: The righteous shall shine as the lily.

General Observations

Imitation is less formalized and restrictive in this music than it is in, say, the Baroque fugue. Most works begin on tonic or dominant notes. Imitation may occur at any pitch interval, though most often at the fifth, fourth, or octave (above or below). It may continue for only a few beats or through an entire section or work (strict canonic imitation). The time and pitch intervals often change in mid-phrase. Tonal or real responses (answers) are possible, though the latter are generally preferred. In a tonal response, the leap of a fourth at or near the head of the leader is answered by a fifth at the comparable point in the follower. Likewise, a fifth is imitated by a fourth. Thus, a leap from tonic to dominant can be answered by a leap from dominant to tonic, and vice versa. In a real answer, the intervals remain the same for leader and follower, though a major interval may be answered by a minor, or a minor by a major. Some tonally adjusted answers are given below.

Example 75

Mirror imitation is not uncommon in this style. Here, the follower is a melodic inversion of the leader.

Example 76

Stretto imitation, in which the follower enters before the leader has completed its statement of the theme, is very common. Considerable overlapping of themes is the result, as can be seen from the following example:

Example 77

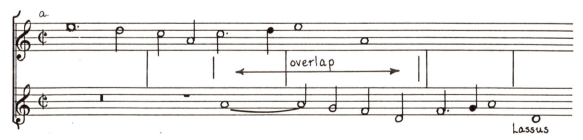

Some voice-crossing may result if the pitch interval of imitation is small, especially if the theme contains large skips. Thus, the imitation of wide-ranging melodies at close intervals is normally avoided. Note the partially inverted answer in the following example.

Example 78

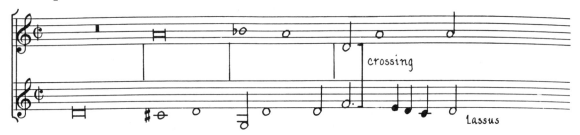

The answering voice usually enters on the comparable beat to the leader, either weak or strong. Thus, a theme beginning on beat one is answered on beat one or beat three, as in example 79. The only exception to this procedure is stretto imitation at one or three beats.

Example 79

Exercises

1. In the following exercises, try systematically to find *all* the workable answers to the given themes. Begin by trying imitation at the unison at two beats, then four, six, and eight beats distance, continuing the imitation for at least six beats. Then try imitating at the fourth and fifth, both above and below, at the various beat distances. Finally, try imitation at the other pitch intervals, up to the octave. The answer may enter forming a consonance, or it may create a suspension against the leader if the potential for it is present, as below:

If the imitation seems to be working out well, then continue both voices in strict canon, breaking the canon just before the cadence. Tonal or real responses (answers) are acceptable, but prefer real answers where possible. Try to preserve a regular rhythmic flow, so that both voices are never static at the same time.

Themes for imitation:

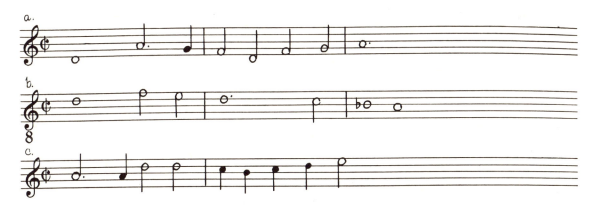

2. Compose a complete section of a motet, for two adjacent voices, using the usual quadruple meter, an imitative opening, and a mode assigned by the instructor. Be attentive to flow, shape, and approach to cadence. The motet section should be about eight to ten measures long, and it should end in an authentic cadence. The following text fragments may be used:

(a) Mìserére nobis (Have mercy on us)
(b) Dóna nóbis pácem (Give us peace)
(c) Hosánna in excélsis (Glory in the highest)
(d) Laudáte dóminum (Praise the Lord)

3. Review the techniques of text setting in *Beatus homo* and *Oculus non videt*, the two-voice motets of Lassus. Then compose a complete two-voice motet, based on one of the following texts, using some text repetition. Begin each section imitatively. The following suggested formats are taken from works by Palestrina and Lassus.

		MODE	MEASURES	CADENCE	FINAL
a.	Benedíctus qui vénit in	Mixolydian	1–8	authentic	D
	nómine Dómini.		9–20	authentic	G
	(Blessed is he who cometh in the name of the Lord.)				

	MODE	MEASURES	CADENCE	FINAL
b. Et in térra pax homínibus bónae vòluntátis.	Dorian	1–8 9–14	authentic authentic	A D

(And on earth peace to men of good will.)

	MODE	MEASURES	CADENCE	FINAL
c. Kýrie eléison Kyrie eleison Kyrie eleison.	Ionian	1–6 7–12 13–20	Phrygian authentic authentic	A G C

(Lord have mercy on us.)

Invertible Counterpoint at the Octave

Sing and discuss the two motet phrases below (Examples 80 and 81). Notice that in the second example the melodic materials have been exchanged between the voices so that what was above is now below. This is referred to as double or invertible counterpoint (a reference not to melodic inversion, but to the exchange of voices). Invertible (double) counterpoint is a technique common in many types of polyphonic music.

Example 80

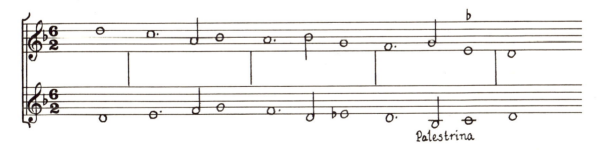

Palestrina

Example 81

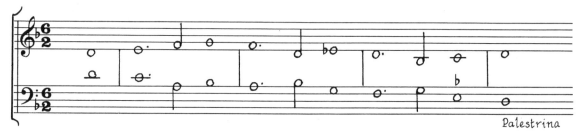

Palestrina

The examples above use invertible counterpoint "at the octave," which means that one of the two voices has been transposed by an octave across the other voice. Observe that under these conditions an octave between the voices in the original becomes a unison, a sixth becomes a third, and so on. Each interval plus its inversion will add up to nine (1 + 8 = 9, 3 + 6 = 9). A table of the results of invertible counterpoint at the octave is given below.

$$\begin{array}{ll}\text{Original interval:} & 1\ 2\ 3\ 4\ 5\ 6\ 7\ 8 \\ \text{Inverted, becomes:} & 8\ 7\ 6\ 5\ 4\ 3\ 2\ 1\end{array}$$

All intervals remain of the same general type (perfect or imperfect consonance, or dissonance) except for the fifth, which becomes a fourth, and which therefore must be treated as if it were dissonant:

Example 82

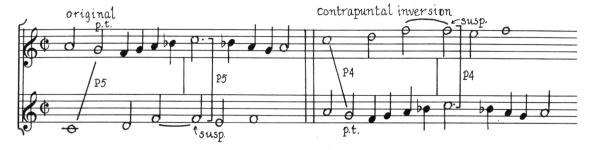

In writing the exercises that follow, observe the following suggestions:

1. In the original, do not exceed an octave between the voices, as this will cause crossing in the inverted version.

2. Each voice should be kept within an octave range.

3. The perfect fifth must be treated as a dissonance in the original, best as a passing tone or suspension, as above.

4. The usual authentic cadence figures work out well, as the 7–8 becomes 2–1.

Example 83

5. Avoid strong-beat unisons except at cadence points. A preponderance of thirds and sixths will result.

6. Suspensions that will work well in inversion are the 7–6 (becomes 2–3), the 4–3 (becomes 5–6) and the 2–3 (becomes 7–6).

Example 84

Exercises

1. Memorize the chart of inversions for invertible counterpoint at the octave. What is the main "problem interval"? Which suspensions work best?

2. Add a voice in invertible counterpoint at the octave above and below the following lines. Try writing just a few notes at a time, checking the inverted result as you proceed, but do not let the resulting line suffer as a melody. It will probably be best to work on three staves, with the original line in the middle.

3. Write several passages of eight to twelve measures in two adjacent voices in double counterpoint at the octave. Some passages should be imitative, or at least briefly imitative at the opening. Texts may be used and a variety of modes may be employed. The counterpoint may become noninvertible shortly before the final cadence.

Invertible Counterpoint at the Twelfth

In this common type of invertible counterpoint, one voice is transposed up or down an octave; the other voice is transposed by a fifth in the opposite direction, crossing the first voice.

Example 85

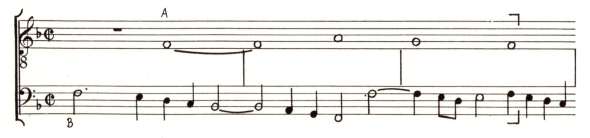

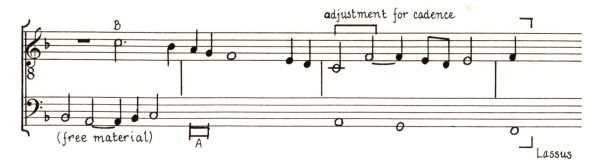

A chart of the intervallic results of inversion at the twelfth follows.

Original interval: 1   2   3 4 5 6 7 8 9 10 11 12

Inverted, becomes: 12 11 10 9 8 7 6 5 4   3   2   1

Each interval plus its inversion totals thirteen. As with invertible counterpoint at the octave, most of the intervals remain in the same general class of dissonance or consonance, except that the sixth becomes a seventh and must therefore be treated as a dissonance.

This technique, while quite commonly used, is rarely sustained for long passages. It is wise to keep each voice within the range of a twelfth and not to exceed an interval of a twelfth between voices, in order to avoid crossing. The only usable suspensions are the 2–3 (11–10 or 4–3) and the 4–3 (9–10 or 2–3).

Example 86

Exercises

1. Memorize the chart of inversions at the twelfth given above. Which is the main problematic interval? Which suspensions work best?

2. Add a voice in invertible counterpoint at the twelfth to lines a through d below. Try writing just a few notes at a time, checking the inverted result as you proceed, but do not let the resulting line suffer as a melody. It may be best to work on three staves, with the original line in the middle.

3. Write passages of eight to twelve measures in two adjacent voices in invertible counterpoint at the twelfth. Some passages should be imitative, or at least briefly imitative at the opening. Texts may be used, and a variety of modes may be employed. The counterpoint may become noninvertible shortly before the final cadence.

Three-voice Counterpoint Chapter 3

SING THE *Benedictus* from Palestrina's *Missa Gabriel Archangelus* below and the other three-voice works in the Appendix. Discuss them in detail, with special attention to the following questions of texture and form, harmony, style, and technique:

1. Are these three-voice works any more or less linear than the two-voice works we have been studying? Is there more textural variety? Do all three voices sing all the time? Discuss text divisions and text setting, including repetition of words or phrases. Where and of what types are the cadences? How is the motion carried over the cadential points? Analyze all points of imitation. How long is the imitation carried out? Is the imitation tonal or real? What are the pitch and time intervals between the entrances? Prepare a graph of the form, as suggested on page 129. Is there any invertible counterpoint? How are the voices kept separate and distinct from each other? Does any one voice predominate? Are there any accompanimental figures? Is the lowest voice purely harmonic (supportive)? Prepare a rhythm graph (of note values), as on page 46, and discuss the interrelations of micro- and macrorhythm.

2. What kinds of chords are present, including chord types (qualities) and inversions? Is functional (Roman numeral) analysis helpful or not? What intervals are present on each beat between each pair of voices? What dissonances are present and how are they treated? What cadential idioms do you find?

3. Compared to what you have observed in two-voice counterpoint, what are the differences of style or technique in these three-voice works? Consider form, cadences, text setting, rhythm, line, texture, and so on.

Example 87

MISSA GABRIEL ARCHANGELUS: BENEDICTUS.

Palestrina

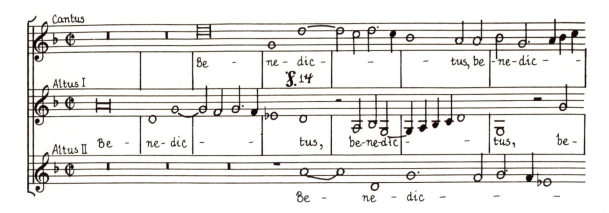

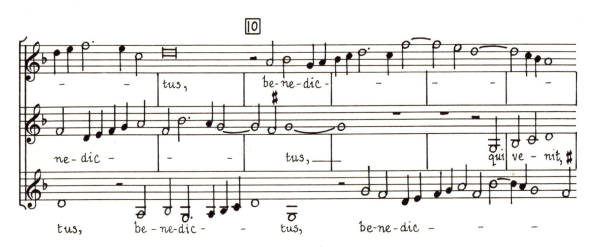

[14]What is the significance of this sign and the one in m. 43?

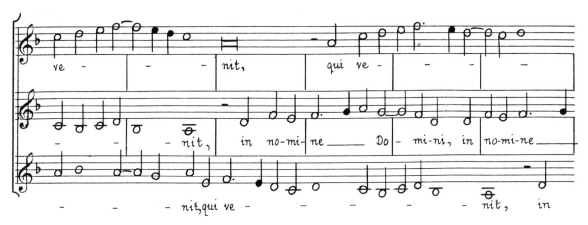

Translation: Blessed is he who cometh in the name of the Lord.

General Observations

Counterpoint in three or more voices is little different in style and technique from that in two voices. The main distinctions, obviously, are in texture and harmony. The fuller texture may lead to a slight simplification of line, and a lessening of the microrhythmic activity. The harmony becomes fuller and more explicit. Otherwise, the techniques are essentially the same. The following are some specific style characteristics of three-voice counterpoint.

Texture and Rhythm

VOICE-CROSSING.   Voice-crossing is not uncommon in three-voice counterpoint, especially between equal upper voices. The lower voices may cross for short passages, but it must be remembered that this will create a new bass line against which to calculate the upper voices. Brief crossings are often an aid to the line, and provide a subtle coloristic change. See especially the motets on pages 150 ff. for typical examples of tenor-bass crossing.

SPACING.   Rarely are the upper voices more than an octave apart, as this tends to isolate the highest voice. Even the lower pair of voices should not be kept far apart for long, as this tends to create a trio-sonata-like texture foreign to this style.

CONTINUITY. Long passages of unbroken three-voice texture are to be avoided, so as to reserve the fullest texture for the final section. Rests usually precede the entrance of a voice that carries thematic material. A voice will often drop out at or just before an internal cadence and re-enter immediately thereafter as a means of weakening its finality and insuring rhythmic continuity and thematic overlap. All three voices usually cadence together, sometimes with a 4–3 suspension into the third of the final triad.

Example 88

CADENTIAL OVERLAP

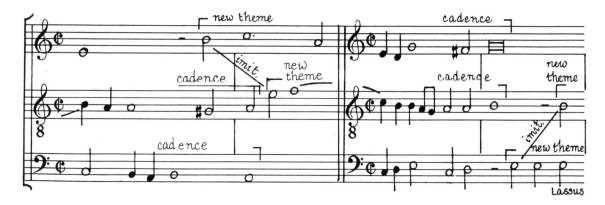

RELATIVE MOTION. Direct (hidden) octaves and fifths can be found in three-voice counterpoint but they rarely involve both outer voices. Direct octaves and fifths sound best when one voice moves by step. All three voices should never leap simultaneously in the same direction, and the outer voices should never leap in the same direction by a large interval. When all three voices move in the same direction, parallel fifths or octaves may result. An occasional brief passage of *fauxbourdon* (parallel first-inversion triads) may be found. There is rarely any preponderance of parallel motion in any pair of voices.

The following are examples of direct fifths:

Example 89

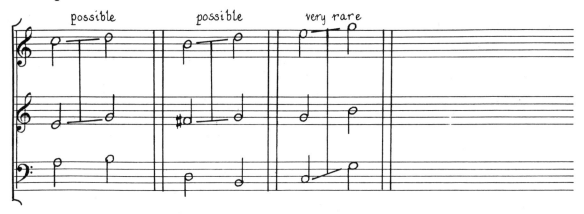

VOICE FUNCTION.   While the three-voice texture is fuller, it is scarcely less linear. Homophonic passages in three voices are more common than in two voices, but imitation still predominates. Strict imitation is often carried out for a few notes only—this is called "head-imitation". There is equality of voice function, although the lowest voice tends to behave in a functional way at cadence points:

Example 90

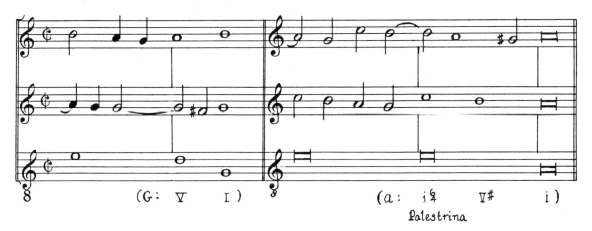

Example 91

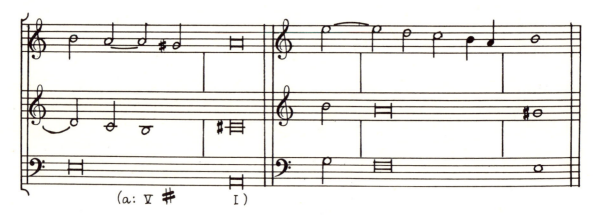

(a: V ♯   I)

RHYTHM.   All three voices rarely move together for long in the same note values, except in passages in familiar style. Short notes in all three parts at the same time are rare, except in climactic, melismatic sections.

Harmony

Review the general comments concerning harmony given on pages 17-30. Since the harmony in three-voice counterpoint is more explicitly triadic, though not really more functional than in two voices, it requires special commentary.

INTERVALLIC RELATIONSHIPS.   On beats one and three each upper voice is consonant with the lowest voice, with the exception of the suspension. The relationship between the lowest and upper voices may in fact be thought of in terms of the criteria for two-voice counterpoint. The two upper voices may form a fourth, if both agree with the lower:

Example 92

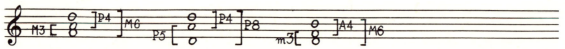

Two voices that move at the same time are usually consonant with each other, unless one is clearly heard as having nonharmonic material (usually a passing tone, a neighboring tone, or a cambiata):

Example 93

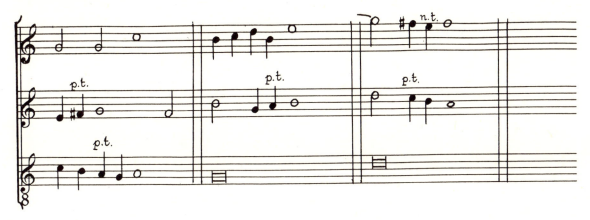

Generally, the longest note sounding at any given time tends to be heard as consonant, and the other voices should be measured intervallically against it.

CHORDS.[15] Any note, including the available accidentals, may form a part of a triad, although B minor, B♭ augmented, and E♭ augmented triads are very rare. Major and minor triads in root position and first inversion form the bulk of the harmonies, but major and minor triads in second inversion ($^6_4$ position) are also found under special cadential conditions (see page 96). Diminished triads in first inversion are used sparingly. The very rare augmented triad, found mainly in English music of the period, is not a stable chord, as it results from a combination of passing or suspensive dissonances:

[15]Review pages 29-30.

Example 94

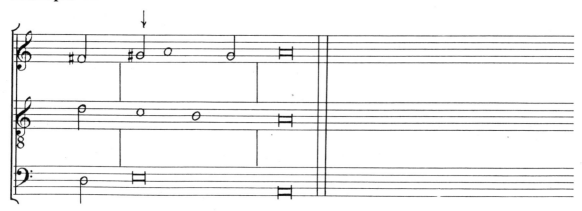

The equally rare root position diminished triad is likewise not a stable chord, but the result of linear activity:

Example 95

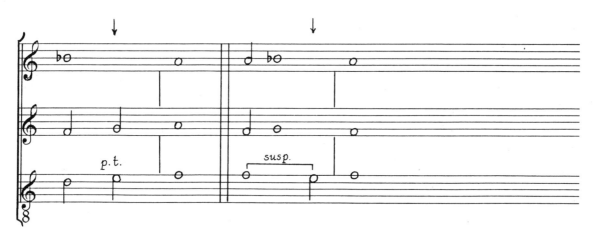

Most works begin imitatively with one voice, or with a complete root position triad on the modal final. The last chord may be a complete major triad (using an accidental as needed to raise the third), a unison on the final, or a triad with third or fifth omitted. Complete major or minor triads predominate, especially on strong beats. Triads with the third omitted are fairly rare by the middle of the sixteenth century. Two voices may be in unison, but all three will have a unison only on the final note.

A first-inversion seventh-chord effect (the $\frac{6}{5}$ chord) occurs occasionally, though it is best not thought of as a real seventh chord. It is usually found at cadences, on a strong beat; often it forms part of a ii$\frac{6}{5}$-V-I cadential progression.[16] The fifth above the bass is usually prepared as a suspension.

Example 96

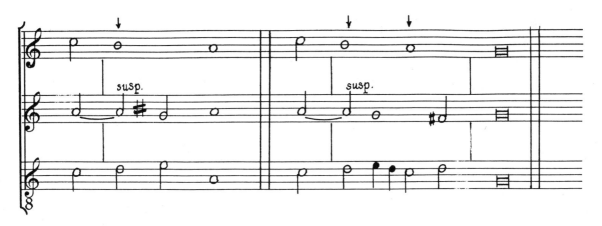

Other seventh-chord effects are also the result of nonharmonic activity in an upper voice and should not be considered chordal units in the same sense as are triads.

[16]Roman numerals are used here only for easy reference. Composers of the time thought in terms of combinations of intervals, not chordal entities.

Example 97

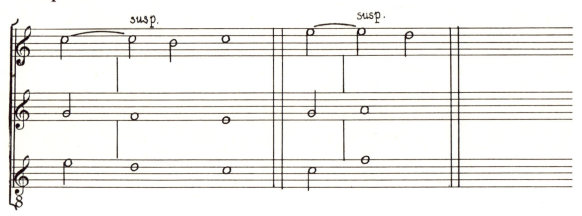

The so-called "consonant fourth," or "consonant $\frac{6}{4}$," is a special idiom. Like many other special figures, it is cadential and usually occurs as follows:

Example 98

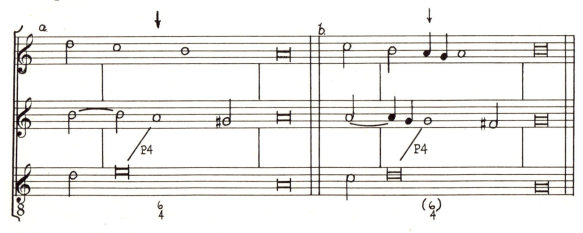

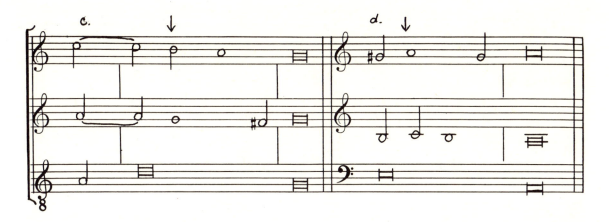

The fourth, it will be observed, falls on a weak beat, is approached by step (usually from above), and is followed immediately by a 4–3 suspension over the dominant note in the lowest voice. It may, as in Example 98b above, be momentarily doubled. It is often preceded by a $^6_5$ sonority. This idiom is clearly the forerunner of the cadential $^6_4$ chord.

DOUBLING.   Any note except the leading-tone may be doubled, although generally accidentals are rarely doubled. Two-voice unisons are common, and three-voice unisons (or octaves) may occur on the final note. A doubled root plus the third is a typical sonority. In any case, considerations of line take precedence over doubling.

Dissonance Treatment

In general, the two upper voices may be dissonant against each other if each is treated correctly with regard to the lowest voice. Similarly, two moving voices may be dissonant if both are treated correctly in terms of a third, more stationary, voice. In composing, to insure proper dissonance treatment and the absence of forbidden parallels, each voice must be calculated and checked against each other voice.

There are a number of characteristic dissonant idioms in three-voice counterpoint.

1. Pairs of passing tones moving simultaneously are consonant with each other. They may move in parallel or contrary motion.

Example 99

2. Eighth notes moving together in two voices will be consonant with each other, although either may be dissonant against the remaining voice.

Example 100

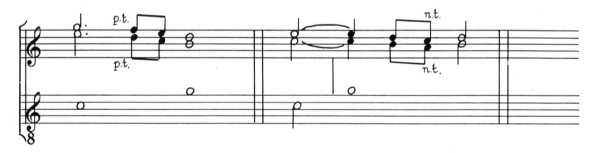

3. Double anticipations (*portamenti*), formed by the two upper voices are always consonant with each other.

Example 101

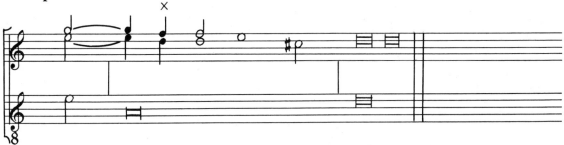

4. The single anticipation may be dissonant against the other voices in quarter notes. The dissonant combination of an anticipation in one voice and a lower neighbor in another is fairly common.

Example 102

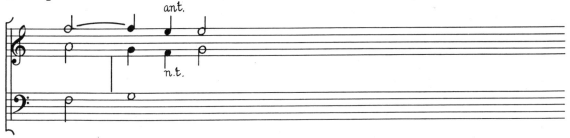

5. The only new suspension idiomatic to three-voice writing is the 9–8 (2–1). Note that the suspension and its resolution are always a *major* second apart.

Example 103

Two voices may suspend simultaneously. With such double suspensions a change of bass is rare. Chains of suspensions are also rare in this music. Typical double suspension combinations are the 9–8 suspension with the 4–3 suspension, the 9–8 with the 7–6, and the 4–3 with the 2–1.

Example 104

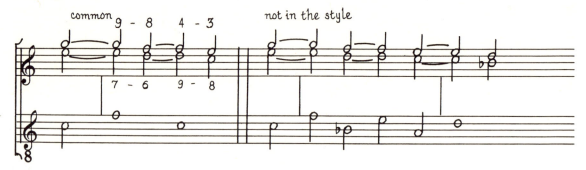

The combination of a 7–6 suspension with a 4–3 suspension is rare, as it produces ineffective parallel fourths.

Example 105

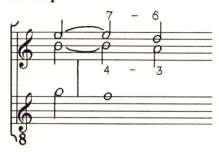

Example 106 illustrates some typical suspension idioms. Notice that the 2–3 suspension at a cadence may resolve to a root position diminished triad, that the 7–6 suspension normally resolves into a first-inversion triad, and that the 4–3 suspension occurs more often at cadences than elsewhere. While the fourth in the 4–3 suspension is usually perfect, it may occasionally be augmented.

Example 106

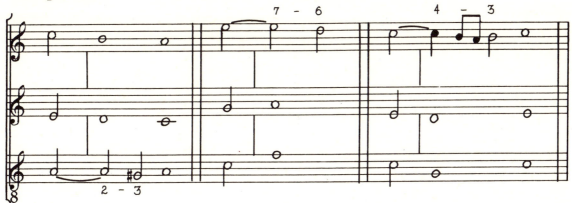

The suspension and its note of resolution will occur simultaneously only when they are a *major* second (or ninth) apart, never a minor second or ninth.

Example 107

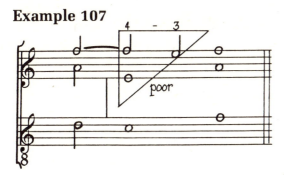

Moving voices are usually consonant with the resolution:

Example 108

Cadential Idioms

The following are some of the standard cadential figurations used in three-voice counterpoint. They should be studied and used as models in your writing.

Example 109

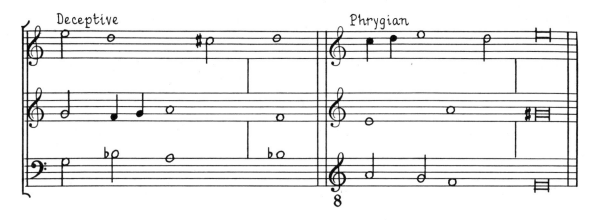

Imitation

Sing and examine again the *Benedictus* from the *Missa Gabriel Archangelus* and the motets on pages 144-155 of the Appendix. Discuss the imitation found in these motets. How far is it carried out? At what pitch and at what time intervals? Is the imitation real or tonal? In what order do the voices enter? Is there invertible counterpoint, and if so, at what intervals? Does the third voice enter in the same time relationship to the second voice as the second voice did to the first?

Comments on Three-voice Composition

Imitation in three-voice counterpoint is not greatly different from that in two. When writing in this style, try to keep each entering voice out of the way of the other voices around it, to insure that it will be heard. Excessive regularity in the order of entries is to be avoided. To achieve variety a different order than the initial one might well be used in subsequent imitation-points. Similarly, the entries ought not be mechanically spaced in time. Often, the third entry will be farther from the second than the second was from the first (see the Appendix, pages 146 and 151, for examples of this). If the first voice enters on beat one, the second voice often enters on beat three. The third entry often creates a complete triad, or a suspensive dissonance.

Example 110

complete triad

susp.

Palestrina   Lassus

The third entry will normally start on the same pitch (though an octave away) as the first, and it will be most effective if it enters on a pitch unused by the other voices just heard.

Triple invertible counterpoint (invertible counterpoint in three voices) is possible. This must be calculated so that all of the six possible arrangements of the voices will be equally satisfactory. The octave is the normal inversion interval. Parallel motion between voices must be handled carefully, because of the potential problem of creating parallel and direct fifths and octaves. Fourths and fifths are best used as passing tones only. Complete triads are also best avoided, because in two of the possible voice arrangements these will be in second inversion. In triple invertible counterpoint a good deal of octave and unison doubling will result. For this reason, extended passages in triple invertible counterpoint are very rare.

Exercises

1. Make a summary of the techniques and devices involved in three-voice counterpoint. In what ways is it freer than counterpoint in two voices? In what ways is it stricter? In three-voice counterpoint what new dissonant intervals are possible and how are they treated? What new suspension idioms are possible? What chord types and positions are possible? How does each voice operate in cadences? In what ways can simultaneous nonharmonic tones in two voices be dissonant against each other?

2. Find the errors of line, counterpoint, text-setting, or formal procedure in the following "motet" and correct these errors.

3. Compose three- to four-measure untexted examples for three adjacent voices (SAT or ATB), that incorporate the idioms listed below:

(a) Three examples of the consonant fourth, in different modes;
(b) The 9–8 and 2–1 suspensions;
(c) Double-suspension idioms: $\begin{smallmatrix}9-8 \\ 7-6\end{smallmatrix}$ $\begin{smallmatrix}6-5 \\ 4-3\end{smallmatrix}$ $\begin{smallmatrix}9-8 \\ 2-3\end{smallmatrix}$ $\begin{smallmatrix}9-8 \\ 4-3\end{smallmatrix}$;
(d) Acceptable direct fifths;
(e) Three examples of the $\frac{6}{5}$ effect at a cadence, in different modes;
(f) Quarter-note passing tones in parallel pairs;
(g) Anticipations in parallel pairs;
(h) Authentic cadences, with the usual nonharmonic tones and ornamentations, in all modes.

Use a fairly simple texture, and employ a variety of modes. Write out these examples neatly and carefully, so that they can be used for reference in your writing.

In writing the exercises below, keep in mind the following suggestions:

(a) Avoid excessive activity in all the voices simultaneously, especially in short note values. Short rests are useful, but do not let a voice rest just before the final cadence. Do not allow all the voices to move in the same direction simultaneously, especially if they move by leap.

(b) Employ the usual cadential figures.

(c) Try to use new devices—the consonant fourth, the $\frac{6}{5}$ effect, the double suspensions, the 9–8 and 2–1 suspensions, and a variety of nonharmonic tone activity.

(d) Be sure not to fall into the habit of thinking harmonically. Think *interval*, not chord function. Sing each line as you work on it, to insure rhythmic interest and flow. Try to work away from the piano, using it only as needed to check your work.

(e) Make sure that no two voices move at the same pace for long. The ideal texture is of three independent voices, with no extended pairing.

(f) Analyze all vertical intervals between each pair of voices and check all dissonances for proper treatment. Check each pair of voices for parallel and direct fifths and octaves.

(g) Perform and criticize all work in class. If some of the following exercises can be done together in class, it will help to clarify the underlying concepts as well as the working process.

4. In the following work, imitations have been started. Fill in the voices where indicated, continuing all imitation points as far as possible before going into non-imitative texture.

Missa Ave maris stella: et resurrexit   *Victoria*

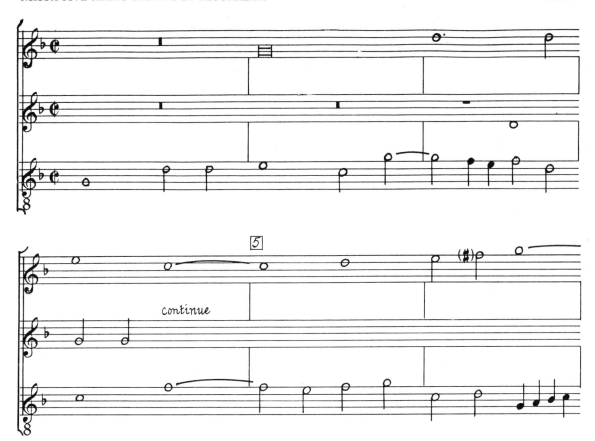

5. (Optional.) To the given voice, add two more voices in triple invertible counterpoint at the octave. Show the result in all six possible voice positions:

$$
\begin{array}{cccccc}
1 & 1 & 2 & 2 & 3 & 3 \\
2 & 3 & 1 & 3 & 1 & 2 \\
3 & 2 & 3 & 1 & 2 & 1
\end{array}
$$

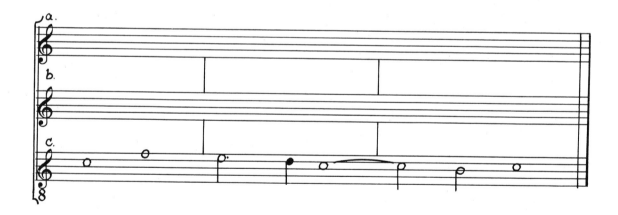

6. To each of the lines given below, add two new voices in mixed note values. The given line should be used successively as the upper, the middle, and the lower voice.

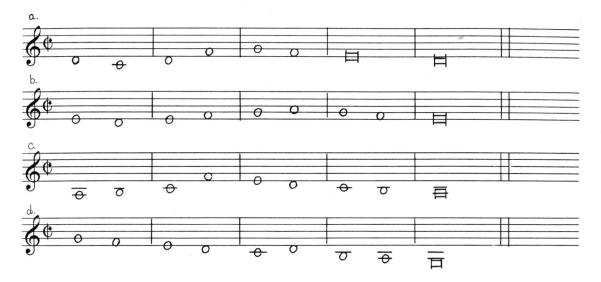

7. Compose eight- to twelve-measure untexted examples of non-imitative counterpoint in three voices, then of imitative counterpoint. Try to write examples with two voices in canon against a free third voice, but keep in mind that the canon should break just before the cadence. Use a variety of modes and voice ranges as suggested by the instructor. Have some examples end with authentic cadences and some with plagal cadences.

8. Below are the opening measures of two works by Victoria. Continue each of these works for eight to twelve more measures, using the same text and ending in an authentic cadence.

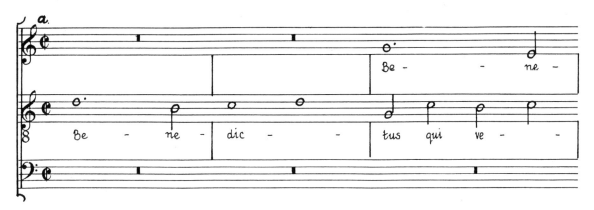

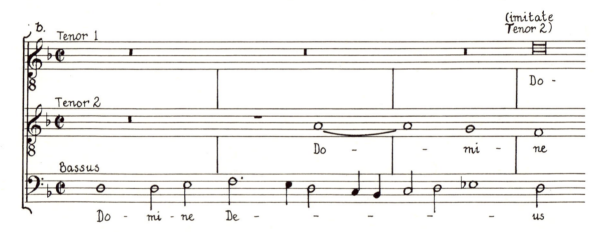

9. Read the background material on the motet (Chapter 5). Using the texts provided in Chapter 5 or texts suggested by the instructor, write motets in three voices. Use a variety of voice ranges and modes, and end at least one motet with a plagal cadence.

Counterpoint in Four Voices   Chapter 4

SING AGAIN THE MOTET *Dies sanctificatus* in Chapter 1 and the other four-voice motets given in the Appendix. Discuss these works, paying particular attention to texture, imitation (order of entries, intervals of imitation, length of imitation, pairing of voices, stretto), harmony, cadences (types, voice leading), and doubling. Note the passages in familiar style (homophony), and analyze chord root movement in these passages. Which kinds of root movement seem most prevalent? To what extent does the harmony admit of functional analysis? What spacings are typical and what spacings are avoided? Does the bass voice function more harmonically than it does in fewer-voiced textures?

Review the general comments on harmony, texture, and form presented in Chapter 1.

General Observations

There are really no additional technical details found in writing for more than three voices. The criteria for effective counterpoint are the same; the main differences are textural. Complete triads occur on most beats, and the final triad is usually complete. In most triads, the root is doubled, although any note that is not the leading tone may be doubled. There is a greater use of homophony—whole sections may be in familiar style. In such sections, the bass may assume a largely supportive function. Imitation tends to be at the octave, fourth, or fifth, and it often involves pairing of voices in stretto, as in the motet *Dies sanctificatus*, measures 1–12. Strict canon is rare, as is lengthy invertible counterpoint.

The harmony is still largely non-functional (in the common practice sense) except at cadences, and there is more root movement by second and third than one typically finds in tonal music. Linearity still takes precedence over considerations of functionality and doubling. Modes are quite freely interchanged by the use of accidentals; Dorian and Aeolian are the modes most often intermixed. Spacing is usually close, with the adjacent upper voices rarely more than an octave apart.

The following cadential idioms typical of four-voice composition are to be analyzed in detail and used as models in your writing. The examples are from the works of Lassus and Palestrina.

Example 111

Authentic (transposed Dorian)

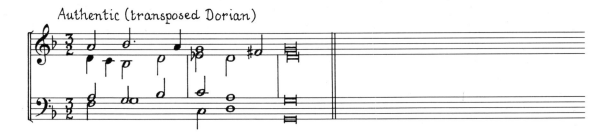

The Motet Chapter 5

SING AND DISCUSS the four- and five-voice motets in the Appendix, paying particular attention to overall form, cadences (finals, types, placement in form), imitation-points, phrase structure (length, overlapping), text setting (mood, emphasis of important words, text-repetition, relation of text divisions to musical form, use of melismas, text-painting, if any), contour (phrase shape and overall climax, if any), texture (contrast between sections, use of homophony, paired imitation and imitative versus non-imitative counterpoint), and rhythm (placement of relatively active sections and use of triple meter). Graph the overall form, using the following format:

Example 112

PALESTRINA: *Dies sanctificatus*

Authentic Cadence (G)

Measure: 5   ∨   10

S ThI(D) Dies sanctificatus illuxit nobis ────────── free 〰〰〰〰〰

A   ThI(G) Dies sanctificatus illuxit nobis ────── free 〰〰〰

           [stretto]

T   ThI(D) Dies sanct . . .

B   ThI(G) Dies . . .

(paired imitation in stretto)

Mode: Mixolydian
Symbols: ThI(D)   Theme one starting on D
   ⎤   Imitation (theme) ends
   ∨   Cadence

General Observations

The sixteenth-century motet (a polyphonic, sacred vocal work, in Latin, normally with a prevailingly imitative texture) is not a form, but a *procedure*. One should be careful not to over-generalize about overall form, but the comments below are true for most motets in the Palestrina style.

The imitative motet (fugal style) is typically based on successive points-of-imitation, and is sectionalized by cadences.[17] Each new phrase of the text has a new theme, treated imitatively by all the voices or homophonically. Motets vary drastically in length, depending on the amount of text set and on the degree of homophony. Some are in one section, others in two or three large sections (called *partes*), demarked by strong cadences. Within each section, cadences are smoothed over by dropping out voices, by thematic overlap, and by suspensions, all of which techniques preserve the flow of the music.

The voices are balanced in rhythmic and thematic importance. One or two important motives often permeate the texture. One section, often the last, may be in triple meter. This may be a contrasting homophonic setting, or an "Alleluia" setting. The last section is often climactic and melismatic. Text-painting of a rather obvious kind (on words such as "ascendit") is typical.

Imitation

Imitation is often found *paired* and at tonic and dominant pitch levels (at the fifth or fourth), as in the motet *Dies sanctificatus*. The opening in particular tends toward these standard tonic-dominant relationships (in Phrygian, the E-A relationship is used). The length of strict imitation varies widely. There is little use of rigorous canonic procedure, although the first pair of voices is often in

---

[17]These generalizations apply fairly well also to most Mass movements, hymns, and offertories.

exact canon until the entrance of the second pair. Often, only the first few notes (the "head" of the phrase) are imitated. Successive entrances are usually staggered metrically, so that a theme on beat one is imitated on beat three. Strictly imitative sections usually break off into non-imitative (free) counterpoint, and imitation usually breaks down with the approach of a cadence. Quadruple invertible counterpoint is not common. In a typical arrangement of thematic materials two themes are exposed simultaneously in the first voice-pair, and the same two themes are imitated by the second pair, as follows:

Example 113

1. S Th. I———⌐ free material ～～～～～～～～～

2. A Th. II - - - - - - -⌐ free material ～～～～～～～～～

3. T   Th. I————————

4. B   Th. II - - - - - - - - - - - - - - -

Voice three will usually begin an octave away from the first pitch of voice one, and voice four enters in the same relation to voice two.

Exercises

1. Add voices as indicated in the following two motets. All important rests have been shown, as well as imitative entrances.

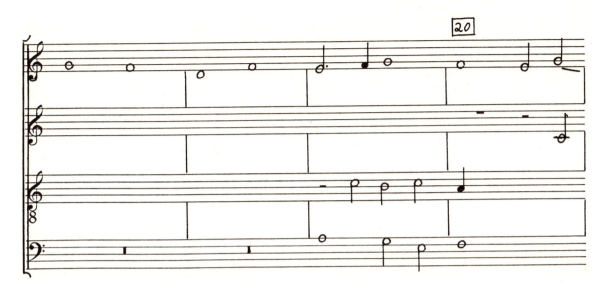

(Phrygian)　　　　　　　　　　(Plagal)

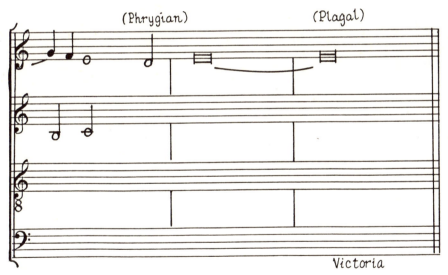

Victoria

THE CRAFT OF MODAL COUNTERPOINT

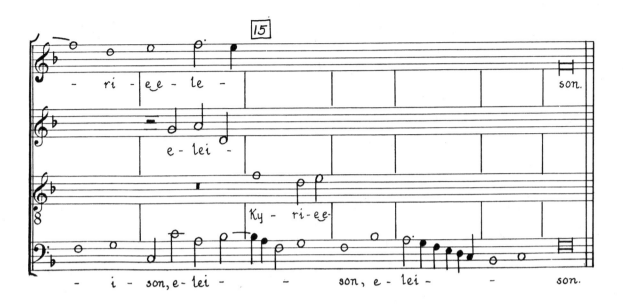

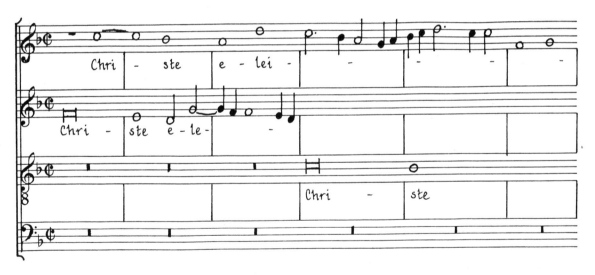

son. Chri-ste e-le-   Chri -

Chri -   ste e - le -

-i-son___   e-le -

Chri - ste e -

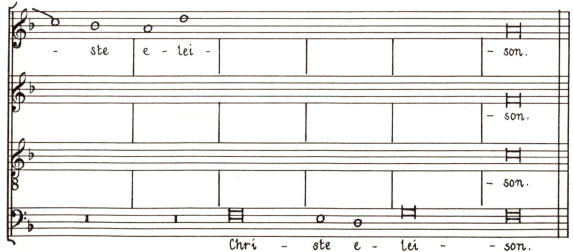

- ste e - lei -   - son.

- son.

- son.

Chri - ste e - lei - - son.

Palestrina

2. Before writing the following exercises in the familiar style, sing and study the homophonic sections of the motets in the Appendix, pages 169-172, and the section on harmony above, pages 92-97.

a. Using an SATB format, add three more voices in familiar style to the given voices. Use mostly root position triads and a simple texture, with a few passing tones and suspensions. There should be few quarter notes and no eighth notes. In $\frac{3}{1}$, suspensions can occur on beats one or two. Some of these exercises should be done in class at the board.

b. Set one of the following texts in the familiar style for SATB. Keeping in mind that these should sound more modal than tonal (functional), limit the use of accidentals and do not over use root movement by fourth or fifth.

Hosána in excélsis [in triple meter] (Glory in the highest)

Véni sáncte spíritus, et emítte cóelitus, lúces túae rádium (Come holy spirit, and send down from heaven the shining of thy light)

Laudáte Dóminum in týmpanis, cantáte Dómino in cýmbalis (Praise the Lord with drums, sing to the Lord with cymbals)

Comments on Motet Writing

Before beginning the following compositional exercises, review carefully all technical and stylistic details. Sing and listen to as much appropriate music as possible until the style becomes a natural mode of expression. No style can be truly internalized by simply memorizing "rules." The following suggestions should be kept in mind as you work on the exercises:

1. Avoid excessively thick spacings and textures. Use rests judiciously and be careful to keep the voices within their proper ranges. Do not allow all the voices to sing either high or low together for long. Short passages in two- or three-voice texture will be a welcome relief, as will passages in the familiar style.

2. The voices should, as always, be independent of each other with respect to phrasing, rhythm, and contour.

3. Avoid squareness of metrical effect in both the microrhythm and the macrorhythm.

4. Do not cadence too often, and be sure to weaken or cover (elide) the internal cadences. The final cadence should be authentic or plagal.

5. Four-voice works are generally longer and more varied in texture than those in fewer voices. Work for textural and metric variety and for a climactic final section.

6. Vary the order of voice entries from one section to the next.

7. Do not let the bass line become merely supportive or the upper voices predominant.

8. A voice that has been resting will often re-enter with the theme.

After you have mastered all aspects of four-voice composition in this style, feel free to move on to composition in five voices, which is technically no different from that in four. Greater freedom is found with regard to fifths by contrary motion and direct octaves and fifths. More note repetition and homophony are typical, and all voices will rarely sing at the same time except in climactic or homophonic passages. For models of five-voice works, see the Appendix, pages 190-213.

Imitation Exercises

1. Continue the motet openings given for eight to twelve more measures, using imitative and then free counterpoint, and ending in a strong cadence.

c.

2. Use each of the voices given below as the basis for a motet section, treating the given voice as a theme for paired imitation. Use stretto between the voices of each pair. Continue the motet section for about twelve to sixteen measures and end in a cadence.

3. Write motets in four voices (SATB), using the following texts or others of your own choosing. In each motet, use a variety of imitative and non-imitative counterpoint, familiar style, melismatic and syllabic setting, and cadence types. The texts have been divided to show the musical subsections. The textual formats show the subdivision of the text as set by each composer, along with the length of each subsection and the cadence type and final with which it ends. In the interest of continuity, all medial cadences (those not at the end) are elided with the phrase that follows. Whether these precise formats are used or not is left to the discretion of the instructor.

	MODE	MEASURES	CADENCE	FINAL
a. Lassus:	Phrygian			
Laudábo nómen Déi		1–12	authentic	A
cum cántico		12–17	authentic	G
et magnificábo éum in		17–31	authentic	C
láude		31–41	plagal	E

(I shall praise God's name in song, and I shall exalt Him with hymns of praise.)

	MODE	MEASURES	CADENCE	FINAL
b. Palestrina:	Aeolian			
Pars méa Dóminus		1–8	authentic	A
díxit ánima méa		8–11	authentic	C
proptérea exspectábo		12–17	authentic	G
éum		18–24	authentic	A

(The Lord is my portion, saith my soul; thus will I await Him.)

	MODE	MEASURES	CADENCE	FINAL
c. Victoria (*prima pars* only):	Transposed Aeolian with Dorian			
O mágnum mystérium		1–9	authentic	D
et àdmirábile		10–19	authentic	G
sàcraméntum		19–25	authentic	D
ut ànimália vidérent		25–28	authentic	G
Dóminum nátum		28–39	authentic	G
jacéntem in praesépio				

(O great mystery and awesome sacrament; that the animals should see the Lord lying in a manger.)

	MODE	MEASURES	CADENCE	FINAL
d. Palestrina (*prima pars* only):	Transposed Ionian			
Sícut cérvus desíderat		1–13	authentic	F
ad fóntes aquárum		13–17	authentic	F
ita desíderat ánima mea		17–23	authentic	F
ad te Déus		23–38	plagal	F

(As the hart panteth after the fountains, so panteth my soul after Thee, O God.)

4. Compose a four- or five-voice motet. Choose a mode and text yourself or use ones suggested by the instructor.

Suggestions for Further Study

Time permitting, the student may wish to undertake one of the following studies. Alternatively, these may be used as end-of-term projects for the entire class.

1. Investigate late sixteenth century secular vocal music. Such a study could focus on national styles, particular forms (the Italian madrigal, the villanesca, for example), or a particular composer or group. Points of similarity and difference in style and technique, as compared to sacred music, should be noted in detail.

2. Study the music of one composer or group of composers of church music, or compare two composers or national styles. (The English style makes an interesting contrast to that of Palestrina.) Or compare the sacred and secular styles of one composer (Lassus, for instance).

3. Analyze settings of the Mass by various composers and draw general conclusions about how each section of the text is normally set. Then compose a four- or five-voice Mass.

4. Study a particular technical aspect, such as the suspension, and trace its treatment from Josquin through Lassus. Or undertake a brief historical survey of the development of the consonant fourth.

5. Study the music of an earlier composer, school, or period, focusing on motet composition, and compare it in detail to the music of Palestrina and his contemporaries.

6. Trace the development of the conservative sacred style after Palestrina, such as in the *prima prattica* works of Monteverdi. Or compare the theoretical writings of the seventeenth or eighteenth centuries, supposedly based on the Palestrina style (as described in the writings of Fux), to the actual music of the Palestrina school.

Appendix

Alleluia

Al - le -lu - ia. Ju - - stus ger - mi - na - - bit. si - cut li - li - - um. et flo - ra - - - bit in - ae - ter - num an - te Do - mi - num.

Alleluia. The righteous will blossom as the lily and will flourish forever in the presence of the Lord.

Kyrie eleison

Ky - ri - e e - le - i - son. Chri - ste e - le - i - son. Ky - ri - e e - le - i - son.

Lord have mercy upon us. Christ have mercy upon us. Lord have mercy upon us.

Agnus Dei

O Lamb of God, that takest away the sins of the world: have mercy upon us. O Lamb of God, that takest away the sins of the world; grant us peace.

Asperges me

Thou shalt sprinkle me, O Lord, with hyssop, and I shall be cleansed; thou shalt wash me and I shall be made white as snow. Have mercy upon me, O God, according to thy great mercy. Glory be to the Father, and to the Son, and to the Holy Spirit. As it was in the beginning, is now and ever shall be, world without end. Amen.

Lassus: Beatus vir

et in sen - su _____ co - gi - ta - - bit cir-

tur, et in sen - su co - gi - ta - - bit

cum-spec - ti - o - nem De - - - i cir - cum-spec

cir-cum-spec - ti - o - nem _____ De - - i cir-

ti - o - nem De - - - - i.

cum-spec - ti - o - nem De - - - - i.

Blessed is the man who will remain in wisdom, and who will exercise himself in justice, and who will meditate within himself on thoughts of God.

Justus cor suum

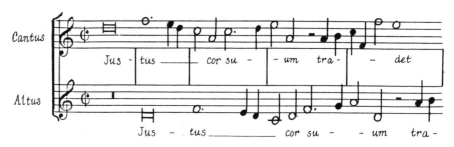

Cantus

Jus - tus _____ cor su - - um tra - - det

Altus

Jus - tus _____ cor su - - um tra -

The righteous man commits his heart to watching at the break of day for the Lord who made him, and in his presence he will entreat him.

Qui sequitur me

He who follows me walks not in darkness, but he will possess the light of life: saith the Lord.

Justi tulerunt spolia

The just have taken up the spoils of the unrighteous, and have sung thy holy name, O Lord, and have also praised thy victorious hand, O Lord our God.

Sancti mei

O my blessed ones, who have waged a battle in this world, I will deliver to you a reward for your labors.

Fulgebunt justi sicut lilium

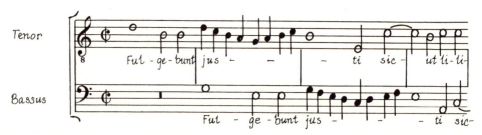

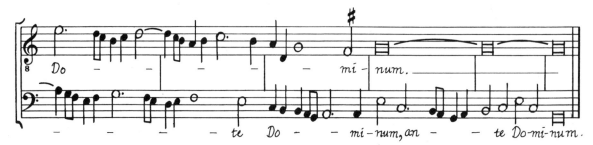

The righteous shall shine as the lily, and will flourish as a rose in Jericho in the presence of the Lord.

Victoria: *Missa Laetatus: Christe eleison*

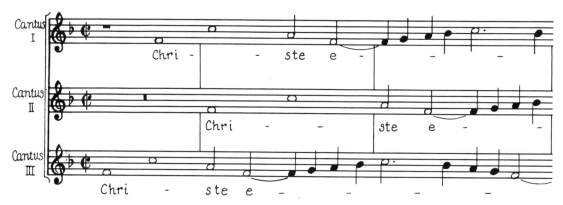

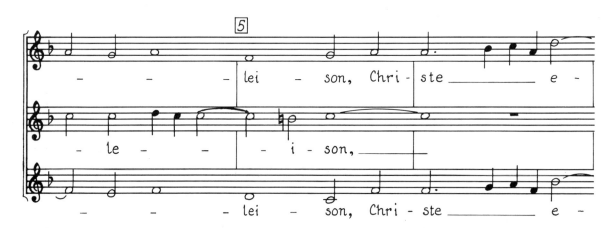

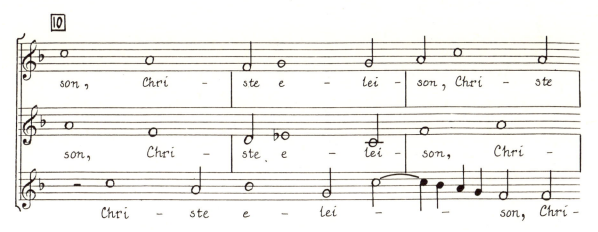

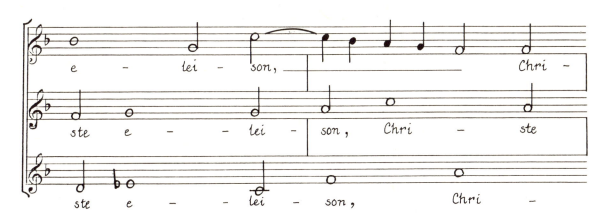

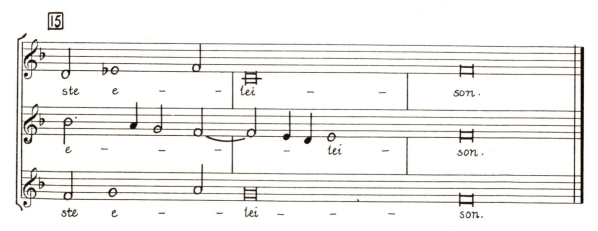

Christ have mercy.

Lassus: *Laudabo nomen Dei*

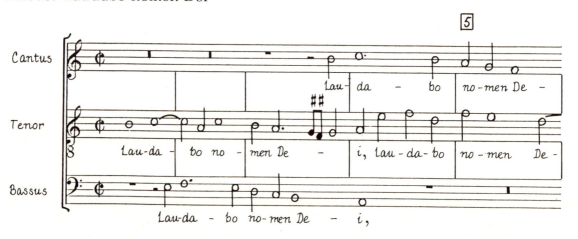

I will praise God's name in song, and I will glorify him in hymns of praise.

Palestrina: *Tu nobis dona fontem lacrymarum*

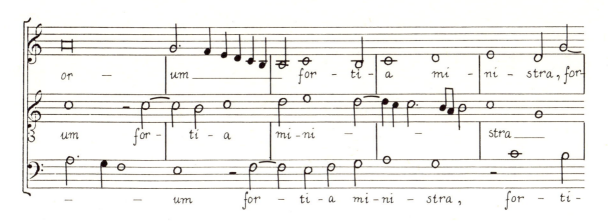

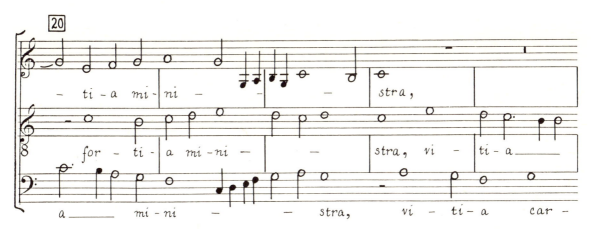

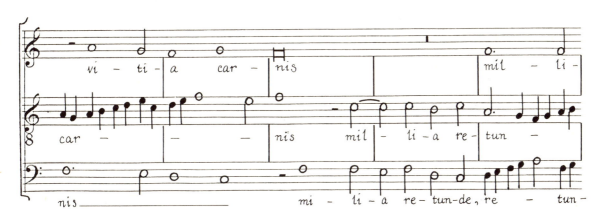

Give thou unto us a fountain of tears, the great strength that comes from fasting; beat back with
your sword a thousand vices of the flesh.

Victoria: *Missa Ave maris stella: Benedictus*

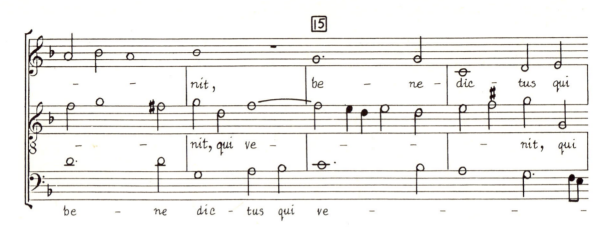

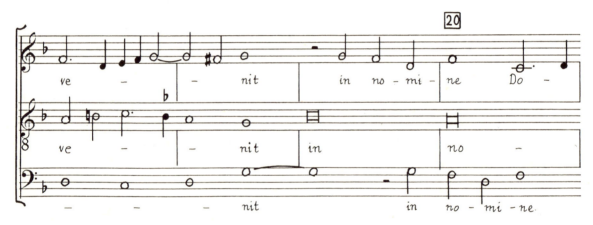

Blessed is he who cometh in the name of the Lord.

Victoria: *O magnum mysterium*

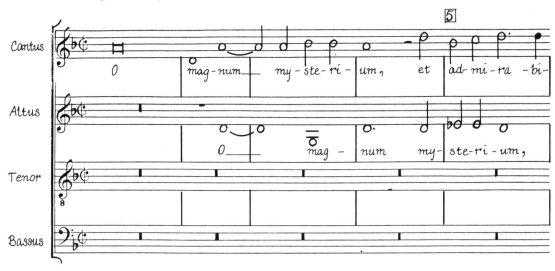

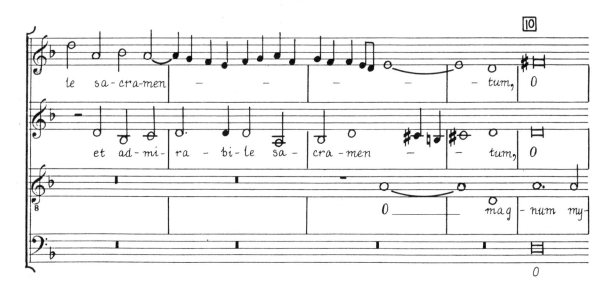

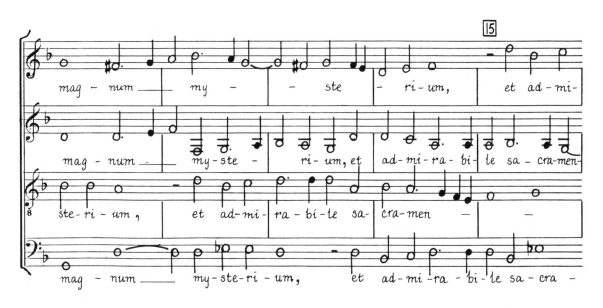

ut a - ni - ma - li - a vi - de - rent Do - mi - num na -

ut a - ni - ma - li - a vi - de - rent Do - mi - num na -

a, ut a - ni - ma - li - a vi - de - rent Do - mi - num na -

a vi - de - rent Do - mi - num na -

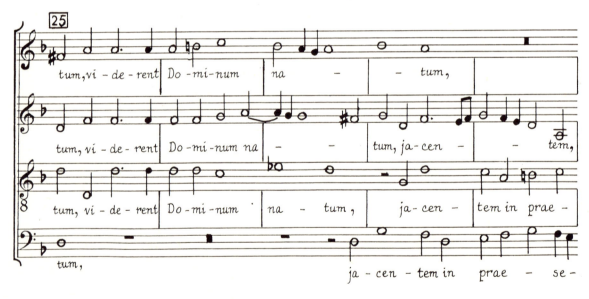

tum, vi - de - rent Do - mi - num na - - tum,

tum, vi - de - rent Do - mi - num na - - tum, ja - cen - tem,

tum, vi - de - rent Do - mi - num na - tum, ja - cen - tem in prae -

tum, ja - cen - tem in prae - se -

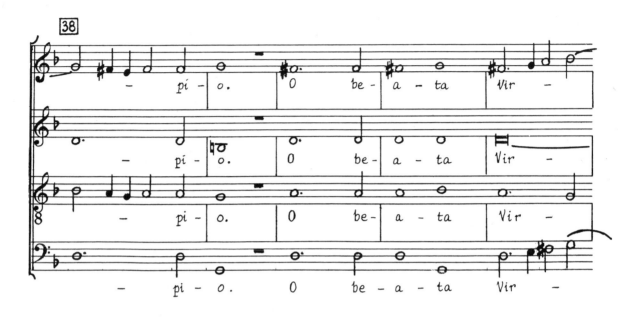

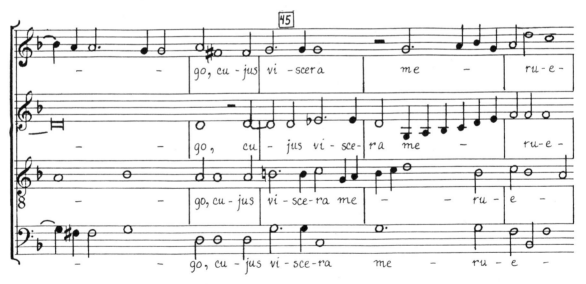

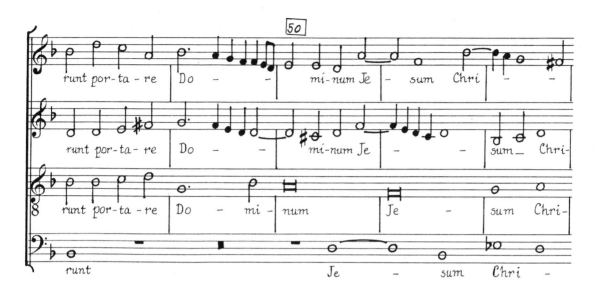

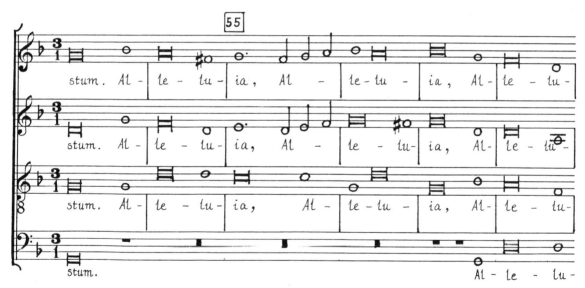

O great mystery and wonderful sacrament, that the animals should see the Lord lying in a manger. O blessed Virgin, whose womb was blessed to bear the Lord Jesus Christ. Alleluia.

Palestrina: *Tollite jugum meum*

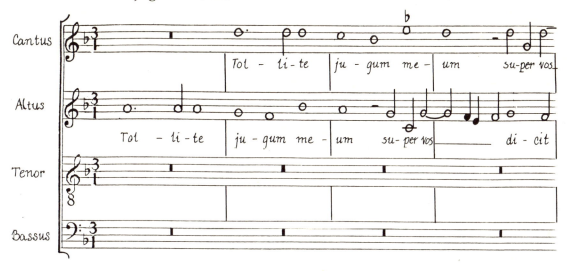

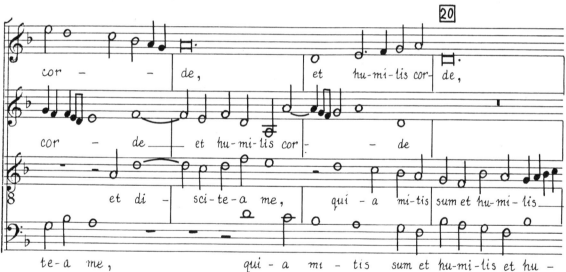

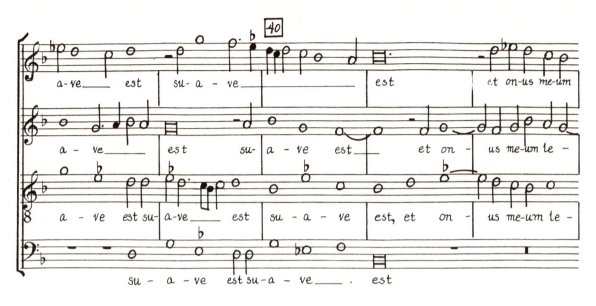

Take up my yoke upon you, saith the Lord, and learn from me, for I am meek and humble of heart; for my yoke is pleasant and my burden is light.

Palestrina: *Veni sancte Spiritus*

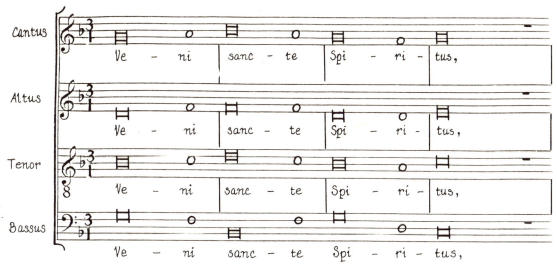

et e - mit - te coe - li - tus Lu - cis

et e - mit - te coe - li - tus Lu - cis

et e - mit - te coe - li - tus Lu - cis

et e - mit - te coe - li - tus Lu - cis

tu - ae ra - di - um.

tu - ae ra - di - um.

tu - ae ra - di - um.

tu - ae ra - di - um.

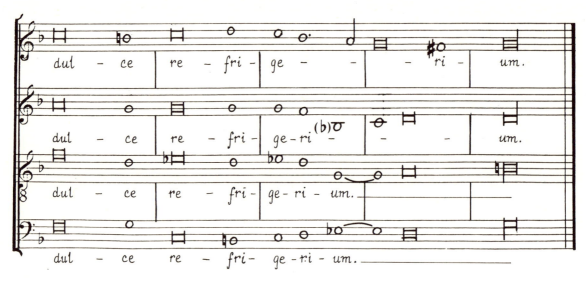

dul - ce re - fri - ge - - - ri - um.

dul - ce re - fri - ge-ri - - - um.

dul - ce re - fri - ge-ri - um.

dul - ce re - fri - ge-ri - um.

Come Holy Spirit, and send down from heaven the shining of thy light. Best consoler, sweet
host and sweet refresher of the soul.

Palestrina: *Sicut cervus*

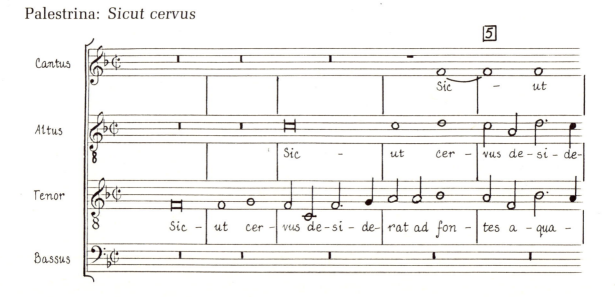

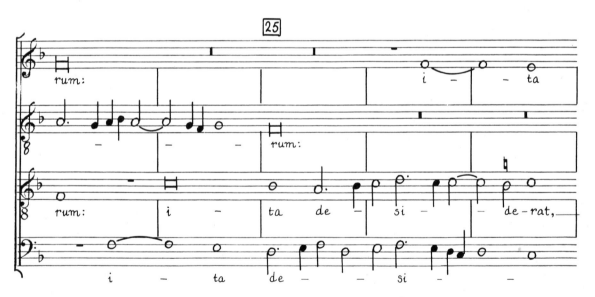

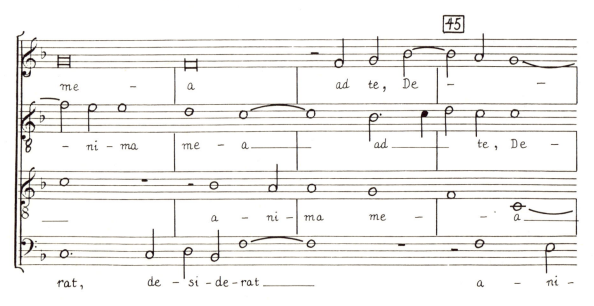

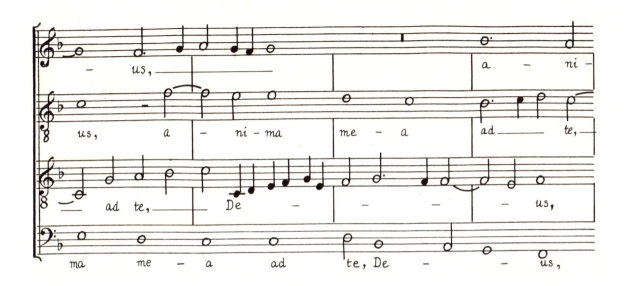

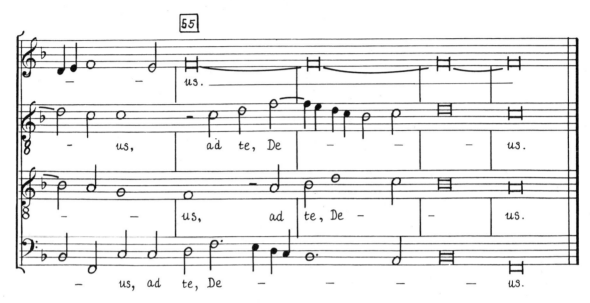

As the hart panteth after the fountains, so also panteth my soul after thee, O God.

Byrd: *O sacrum convivium*

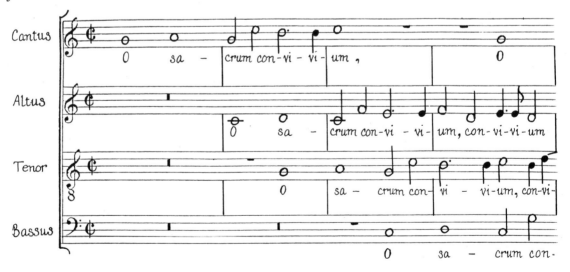

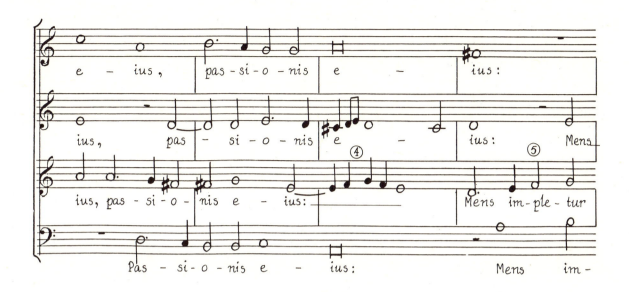

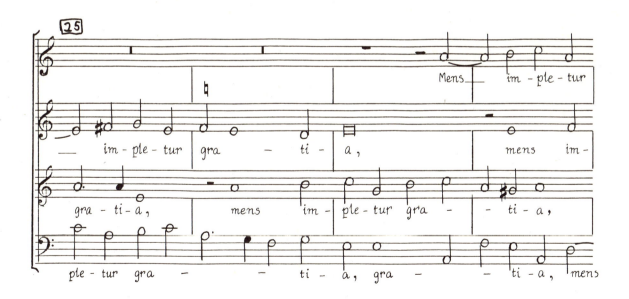

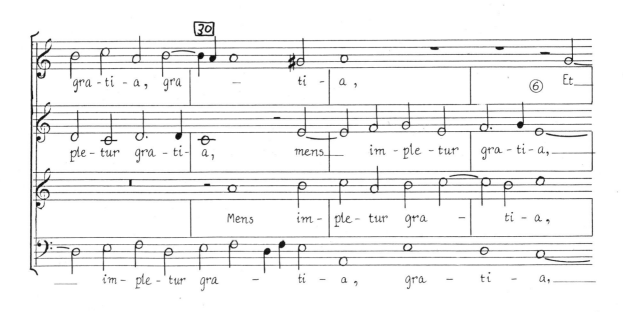

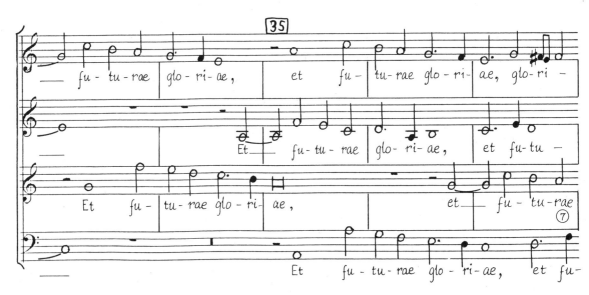

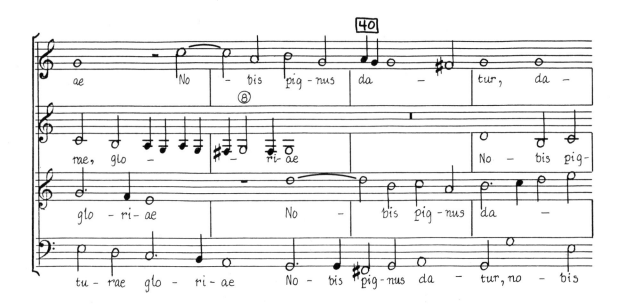

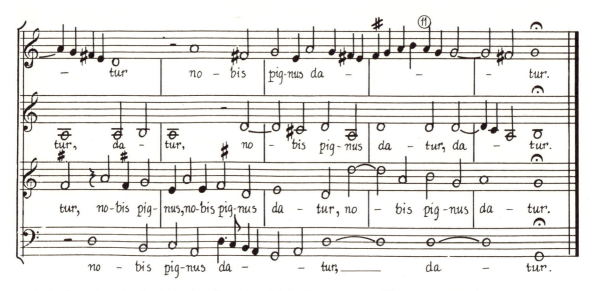

O holy feast in which Christ is taken, in which the memory of his passion is honored anew, in which the mind is filled with thanks, and in which the promise of future glory is given to us.

Byrd: *Ave verum corpus*

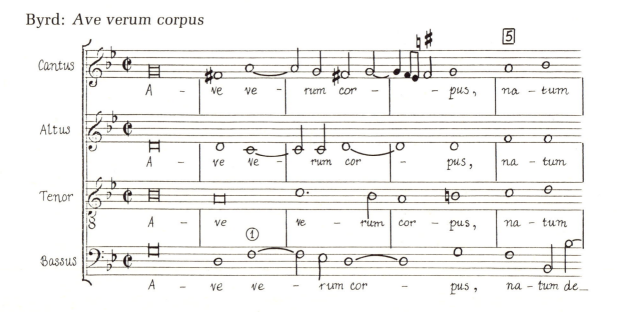

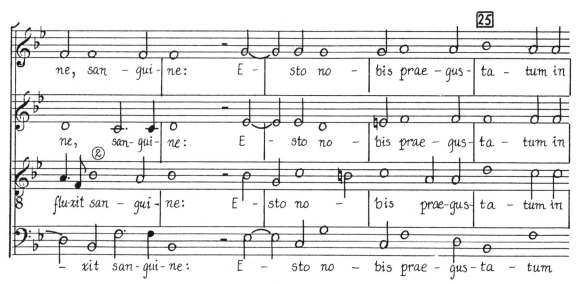

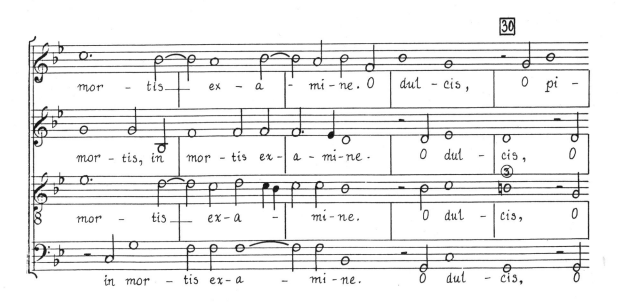

Hail holy body, born of the Virgin Mary, truly having suffered, sacrificed on the cross for man, whose pierced side flowed with water and blood: be for us a foretaste in the trial of death. O sweet one, O holy one, O Jesus son of Mary, have mercy on me. Amen.

Victoria: *Ascendens Christus*

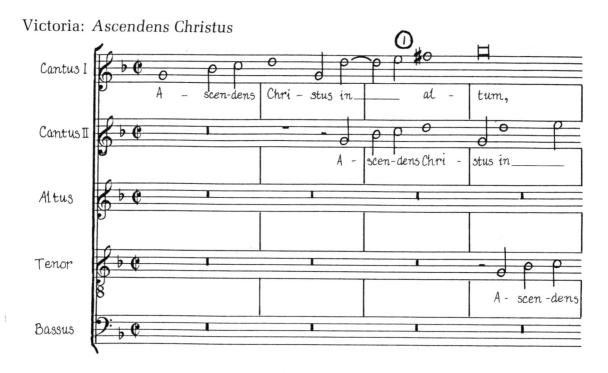

Christ ascending on high, Alleluia, hath led captivity captive, Alleluia. He hath given gifts to men, Alleluia.

Palestrina: *Laudate Dominum*

Praise the Lord, for he is kind; praise his name on the psaltery, for he is sweet. Whatsoever he desired he made in heaven and on earth.

Lassus: *Cum rides mihi*

When you laugh at me, you have withheld a kiss, when you lament to me, you have given a
 kiss. In one kind of sadness, while willing, you are kind; in one kind of happiness, while
 willing, you are harsh.

Victoria: Quem vidistis, pastores?

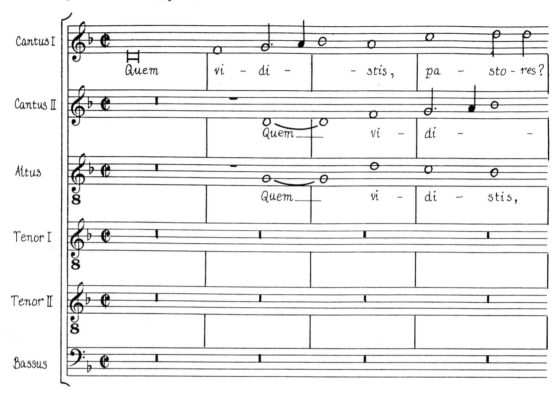

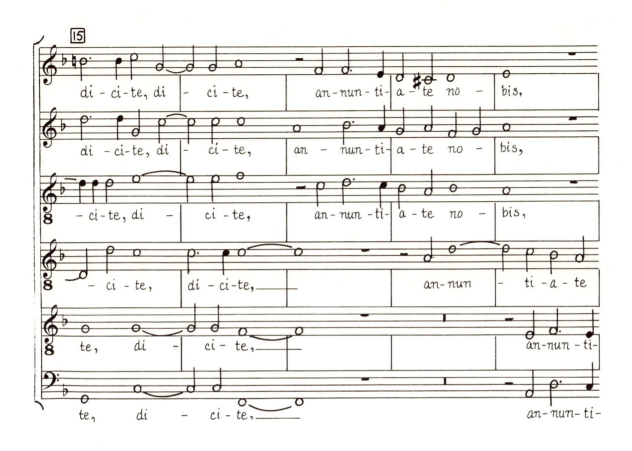

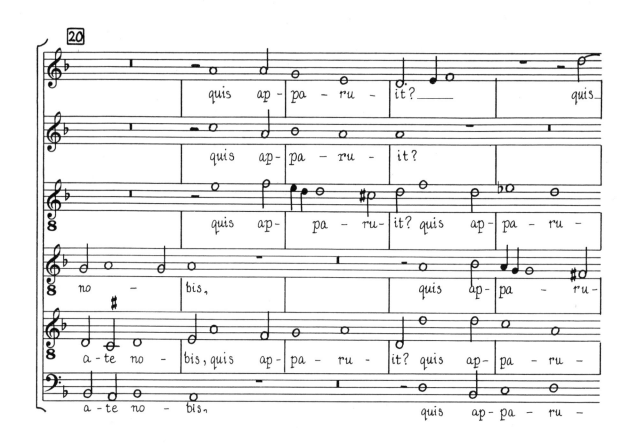

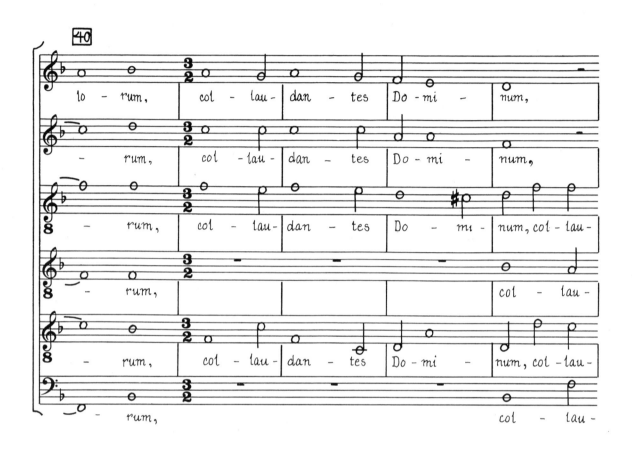

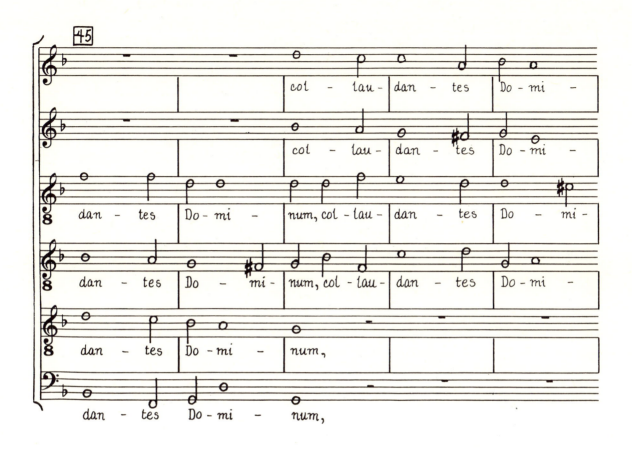

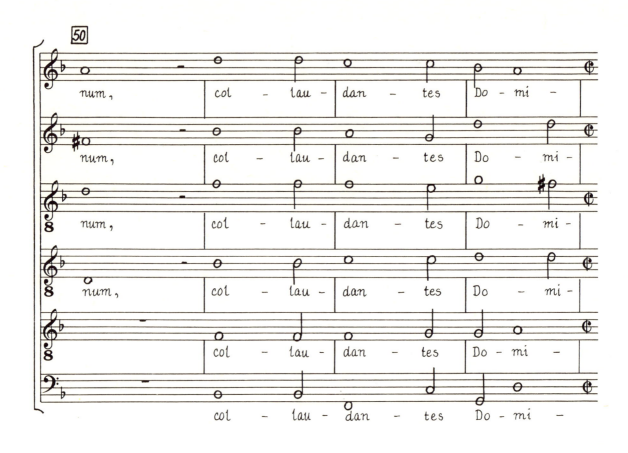

Whom have you seen, shepherds? Tell us, announce to us, who has appeared. We have seen the newborn babe, and the choir of angels praising the Lord. Alleluia.

Bibliography

ANDREWS, H. K. *An Introduction to the Technique of Palestrina.* London, 1958.

APEL, WILLI. *The Notation of Polyphonic Music.* Cambridge, Mass.: The Mediaeval Academy of America, 1953.

HAIGH, ANDREW C. "The Harmony of Palestrina." Ph.D. dissertation, Harvard University, 1945.

HAIGH, ANDREW C. "Modal Harmony in the Music of Palestrina," in *Essays in Honor of Archibald T. Davison.* Cambridge, Mass.: Harvard University Press, 1957.

JEPPESEN, KNUD. *Counterpoint,* tr. by Glen Haydon. Englewood Cliffs, New Jersey: Prentice-Hall, 1939.

JEPPESEN, KNUD. "Palestrina," in *Die Musik in Geschiechte und Gegenwart,* Vol. 10, cols. 658–706.

JEPPESEN, KNUD. *The Style of Palestrina and the Dissonance.* London: Oxford University Press, 1927.

LOCKWOOD, LEWIS, ed. *Palestrina: Pope Marcellus Mass.* New York: Norton, 1975.

MERRITT, ARTHUR TILLMAN. *Sixteenth Century Polyphony.* Cambridge: Harvard University Press, 1944.

MORRIS, R. O. *Contrapuntal Technique in the Sixteenth Century.* Oxford: Clarendon Press, 1922.

REESE, GUSTAVE. *Music in the Renaissance.* New York: Norton, 1954.

SODERLUND, GUSTAVE. *Direct Approach to Counterpoint in the 16th Century Style.* New York: Appleton-Century-Crofts, 1947.

STRUNK, OLIVER. *Source Readings in Music History.* New York: Norton, 1950.